BTEC FIRST

REVISE BTEC

Information and Creative Technology

Unit 1 The Online World

Unit 2 Technology Systems

REVISION GUIDE

Series Consultant: Harry Smith   Author: Karen Anderson

- -

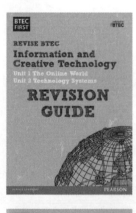

THE REVISE BTEC SERIES

BTEC First in Information and Creative Technology Revision Guide
9781446909799

BTEC First in Information and Creative Technology Revision Workbook
9781446909805

This Revision Guide is designed to complement your classroom
and home learning, and to help prepare you for the external test.
It does not include all the content and skills needed for the
complete course. It is designed to work in combination
with Pearson's main BTEC First series.

To find out more visit:
www.pearsonschools.co.uk/revise

ALWAYS LEARNING   **PEARSON**

Published by Pearson Education Limited, Edinburgh Gate, Harlow, Essex, CM20 2JE.

www.pearsonschoolsandfecolleges.co.uk

Copies of official specifications for all Pearson qualifications may be found on the website: www.edexcel.com

Text © Pearson Education Limited 2014

Typeset by Tech-Set Ltd, Gateshead
Original illustrations © Pearson Education Limited
Cover photo/illustration by Miriam Sturdee

The right of Karen Anderson to be identified as the author of this work have been asserted by her in accordance with the Copyright, Designs and Patents Act 1988

First published 2014

17 16 15 14
10 9 8 7 6 5 4 3 2 1

British Library Cataloguing in Publication Data
A catalogue record for this book is available from the British Library

ISBN 978 1 446 90979 9

Printed in Slovakia by Neografia

Acknowledgements
The publisher would like to thank the following for their kind permission to reproduce their photographs:
(Key: b-bottom; c-centre; l-left; r-right; t-top)

Alamy Images: Finnbarr Webster 43/4, Studio 101 41/6; **Digital Vision:** Digital Vision 17br; **DK Images:** Jane Burton 11cr, Peter Anderson 11c, Vanessa Davies 1/1; **John Foxx Images:** Imagestate 25tr; **Shutterstock. com:** Adem Demir 36tr, Aleph Studio 36cr, Alexander Demyanenko 40/11, Art_man 24tr, 46/2, Baloncici 38r, 42br, bikeriderlondon 6, Blend Images 2, bloomua 58cl, 58cr, Borodaev 40/1, Brian A Jackson 47/8, 55tl, Chad McDermott 44, Chimpinski 40/3, Denis Dryashkin 43/2, Dima Groshev 46/4, florin oprea 43/5, Goodluz 9tr, Herbert Kratky 1/2, hxdbzxy 11br, Iaroslav Neliubov 47/5, jcjgphotography 43/3, kastianz 47/7, Kitch Bain 47/2, Kunal Mehta 42tl, LDprod 1/3, luchschen 40/9, 40b/5, Lusoimages 40/10, 40b/1, mama_mia 1b, Marish. 7tr, 8cr, Masalski Maksim 40/7, 40b/2, megastocker 40/14, Mile Atanasov 47/4, Norman Chan 47/1, Oleksiy Mark 40/4, 51c, phil Holmes 40/15, Photobac 43/1, photofriday 36bl, Rob van Esch 24tc, 46/3, Robbi 40/2, Semen Lixodeev 55tr, SFC 36tl, 42tr, StudioIcon 25tc, 46/5, supergenijalac 38l, vetkit 47/6, Yellowj 30cr; **Veer / Corbis:** Alexander Yurkinskiy 41/5, Brian Jackson 1/4, Cebas 23tl, f9photos 40/12, H2Oone 23br, ilolab 23tr, 25tl, jirkaejc 47/3, Kitch 41/1, Krasyuk Volodymyr 41/4, LCS 40/5, 40b/3, lucadp 41/2, 41/3, luchschen 23bl, Olly 30tr, Pakhnyushchyy Vitaliy 24tl, 46/1, Panagiotis Risvas 36cl, Ronen 40/13, sqback 40/16, StockPhotosArt.com 40/6, 40b/4, terex 40/8, toxawww 45

All other images © Pearson Education

Every effort has been made to trace the copyright holders and we apologise in advance for any unintentional omissions. We would be pleased to insert the appropriate acknowledgement in any subsequent edition of this publication.

Contents

This book covers the externally assessed units in the BTEC Level I/Level 2 First in Information and Creative Technology qualification.

Pearson publishes Sample Assessment Material and the Specification on its website. That is the official content, and this book should be used in conjunction with it. The questions in the *Now try this* sections have been written to help you practise every topic in the book. Remember: the real test questions may not look like this.

Online services 1

Online services are facilities that users can access over the internet and which allow data exchange and interaction. Here are four types of online services:

① Communication

This service is about moving data between users.

Examples include:

- email
- instant messaging
- newsgroups
- social networking (e.g. Facebook)
- online conferencing
- blogs.

② Real-time information

This service is used to get up-to-date information.

Examples include:

- train timetables
- news services
- traffic reports
- flight status updates
- weather.

③ Commerce

This service involves business – buying, selling and money services such as banking.

Examples include:

- internet banking
- online auction websites (e.g. eBay)
- retail sales (e.g. HMV, Tesco.com)
- publishing (e.g. Kindle on Amazon).

④ Government

This service involves public services, such as government bodies, like the DVLA and local council.

Examples include:

- online tax returns
- e-voting
- applications for services or grants
- revenue collection
- renewing car tax.

Worked example

Which **one** of the following is an online commerce service? **(1 mark)**

A ☐ Train timetable   B ☑ Online auction website

C ☐ Online tax return   D ☐ E-voting website

Commerce means 'business' and business is about making money – so commerce services involve money in some way.

Now try this

Which **one** of the following is not a real-time online service? **(1 mark)**

Remember to read questions carefully!

A ☐ Instant messaging   B ☐ Pollen count website   C ☐ Live bus timetable   D ☐ News app

Online services 2

Here are five more online services:

1 Education

This service involves learning and training.

Examples include:

- online learning for learners (e.g. BBC Bitesize)
- online training.

2 Entertainment

This service involves using the internet for leisure and fun.

Examples include:

- online gaming, including multiplayer on consoles and portable devices

- radio players and music websites
- catch-up TV
- on-demand films.

3 Virtual learning environment (VLE) (e.g. Moodle, Blackboard)

This service is a virtual classroom that allows teachers and learners to communicate with each other.

4 Business

This service involves businesses using websites to make their business more efficient or to save money.

Examples include:

- video conferencing (e.g. Skype)

- collaborative working
- business networks.

5 Download services

This service involves files which can be downloaded and saved onto the user's computer. These are LEGAL services.

Examples include downloads for:

- music and film
- software
- upgrades.

Worked example

Which **one** of the following is an online business service?   **(1 mark)**

A ☐ Retail website

B ☐ VLE

C ☐ Online tax return

D ☑ Collaborative working

The online service for business is **not** about businesses using websites for selling. This would be considered Commerce.

Now try this

Give **two** reasons why a user may use download services to acquire software instead of more traditional methods.

(2 marks)

Online advertising

Online advertising is designed to capture and hold the attention of a user to promote a product or service. There are several methods which can be used.

This shows a search engine results page with sponsored (paid for) links.

Google and the Google logo are registered trademarks of Google Inc., used with permission.

Pay-per-click advertising

A web page will host an advert for another organisation. If a user clicks on the advert, they are directed to the advertiser's website. The host will receive payment for each user who clicks on the advert. This is known as an affiliate model.

Banner/Pop-up adverts can be effective in catching users' attention but can also be annoying.

Worked example

Why might a website owner and an advertiser want to be involved with an affiliate model of online advertising? Give **one** reason for each.
(2 marks)

There are two marks – you can give two viewpoints: the host and the advertiser.

A website owner can host an advert and earn money every time a user clicks on it. An advertiser can put their advert on popular websites and potentially get more custom as more users will see their advert.

Now try this

Explain how banner and pop-up adverts aim to capture and retain the interest of web page users.
(2 marks)

3

Online documents – file compression

File compression makes files SMALLER so that they take up less space in computer memory.

Compression is also known as 'zipping' and is done using an algorithm. One file can be compressed or many files can be compressed into one.

File extensions for these include .zip, .rar, .7z and .dmg.

Each file extension is created using a different compression algorithm. Therefore, the user(s) compressing and expanding the file needs to use the same program.

Advantages of file compression

- ✓ Saving memory space on computers e.g. web server
- ✓ Files will upload and download more quickly
- ✓ Files will better fit restrictions, such as the attachment limit on email

Index

When files are compressed, the last item in the compressed file is an INDEX. It contains the information needed to expand the files to their original size.

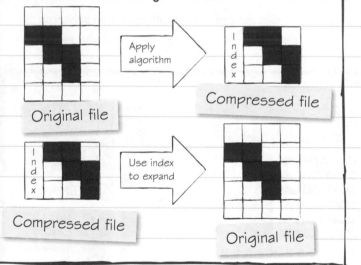

Worked example

Describe how an algorithm and index are used in file compression. **(2 marks)**

An algorithm is used in compression to make the file smaller. An index file is included when the algorithm is used and is part of the compressed file. When the file is expanded, the index holds the information to recreate the original file.

Now try this

Think carefully about all the information the question is asking for.

Sharmeen is sending an email. She would like to attach 3 files which total 27 Mb. Her email's limit is 25 Mb but she does not want to send them separately.

(a) Explain how file compression would help.

(b) Describe the process of compressing and expanding the files. **(4 marks)**

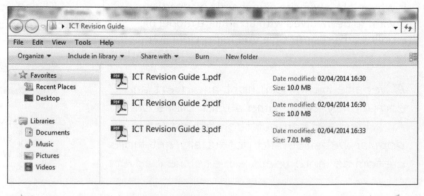

Online software and backups

Traditional software is installed onto a computer whereas online software is accessed over the internet through a web browser.

Advantages of standalone software

✓ As it is installed onto the hard drive, it can be used when there is no internet access.

✓ It runs faster than online software with a poor internet connection.

> User obtains software on DVD or downloads from internet
>
> ↓
>
> User installs software on computer or file server

Online software

Online software is accessed through a web browser and is available anywhere that has an internet connection.

✓ Updated automatically (on the server, rather than on the client)

✓ Backed up automatically

✓ Can be used on different devices (computer, tablet, smartphone, etc.)

✓ Can be used on different operating systems (Windows, Mac, etc.)

Online backups

Backing up files online means saving them to external servers.

✓ If the user's computer fails, the files are saved on servers elsewhere and would still be safe.

✓ Cloud storage is often also backed up so there is double security.

Worked example

> Why is backing up files important? Identify **two** reasons from the list below. **(2 marks)**

A ☑ If files become corrupt

B ☑ If files are accidentally deleted

C ☐ Makes writing and editing easier

D ☐ Makes files easier to find

E ☐ So you can access them anywhere

 Other reasons for backups include viruses.

Backup and restore

If you are backing up a file it is important to make sure that you can RESTORE these files if the original copy is deleted or corrupted. When you are answering questions about backups, make sure you write about making a second copy AND restoring it.

Now try this

> State **two** benefits of using online software, as opposed to standalone software. **(2 marks)**

⬅ Note how many benefits are asked for, and how many marks are available.

Collaborative working online

Collaborative working means people working together. Technology allows collaborative working to happen over the internet. Users can work on the same project or even the same document – and they could be in different countries.

Advantages of collaborative working

✓ Users do not need to travel to work together, saving money, time and the environment.

✓ Users can work on the same document instead of having different versions of the same file.

Version control

This is important so that a user knows which is the most up-to-date document. This is especially important for collaborative working. Version control can be managed by:

- locking the file and making it 'read only' while one user is viewing or editing it
- the software allocating version numbers and dates of editing.

Levels of access

Different users can have different levels of access. This could be set with a username and password. For example, at school or college you will have different access to your teachers on your school network and this is set when you log on.

Login

Username

Password

File permissions

File permissions give users a level of access to specific files.

Read only	Can look at a document but make no changes
Read/Write	Can look at a document and make changes
Full control	Can do anything to a document, including deleting it

It is important to give users training before granting read/write or full control access.

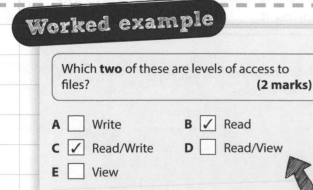

Which **two** of these are levels of access to files? **(2 marks)**

A ☐ Write   B ✓ Read

C ✓ Read/Write   D ☐ Read/View

E ☐ View

There is no permission for 'write' because in order to write, the user has to be able to read the file first.

Keith and Shabina are working on a collaborative document.

(a) Give **one** reason why version control is important. **(1 mark)**

(b) Describe **one** way they ensure version control is used. **(2 marks)**

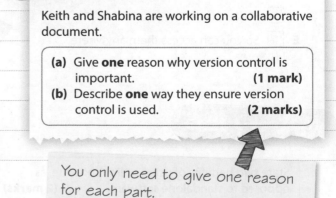

You only need to give one reason for each part.

Online communication 1

Communicating online means transferring data from one user to another or many. Often this is done through specialist software or websites, including social media.

Publishing information

Information can be published online through social media.

Blog	A web log – an online journal or diary
Microblogging	A website or app where short messages are exchanged (e.g. Twitter)
Wiki	A website where anyone can add and edit information
Podcast	Audio or video files which are usually published in episodes
Chatroom	A place on the web where users can communicate, usually through typed words (users online at the same time)
Chat	An exchange of messages, often typed, between users at the same time (in real time)

Sharing information and building communities

SOCIAL NETWORKING sites can connect people with similar interests. Those involved can be in different places.

An ONLINE COMMUNITY is a virtual community (group of people) which only exists online.

It is also known as a NETWORK OF FRIENDS.

Online communities

These often exist in a VIRTUAL WORLD. This is an unreal world which is created by the computer and does not exist in the real world.

Some communities need users to be involved at the same time, such as some online gaming, whereas others can have users interacting at different times, such as a forum or a Virtual Learning Environment (VLE).

Worked example

Virtual Learning Environments (VLEs) are used in schools, colleges and universities.

(a) Give **two** benefits of using a VLE for learners. **(2 marks)**

Learners can submit work through a VLE as a saved digital copy and it can be scanned through plagiarism software and then backed up. They can also create wikis that can be shared with their peers and support learning in their classes.

(b) Give **two** benefits of using a VLE for teachers. **(2 marks)**

Teachers can share resources on a VLE, which means learners and other teachers can access them, such as worksheets, assignment briefs and support materials. They can also access them from school or at home.

Educators can share resources, learners can submit their work and use other tools, such as making quizzes, setting up forums and creating wikis.

Now try this

Describe **two** ways a business could use social networking to enhance their business and make it more profitable. **(4 marks)**

Think carefully about what information the question is asking for.

7

Online communication 2

Communicating online includes instant messaging. Online communication requires rules and involves users in developing a profile for their online presence.

Netiquette

NETIQUETTE is the set of rules to which users should conform when online. It is short for net etiquette. This would include not using capitals (as it means shouting), appreciating privacy and not making unkind comments.

Emoticons

Emoticons, also known as smilies, are images that represent emotions.

Profile

A PROFILE is the online presence of a user in a particular system, for example on a games system or social media website.

The profile will include a name (which may be a pseudonym) and details about the person. It is up to the user how much they reveal and whether they are truthful or not.

An **avatar** is a picture which represents a person, usually as part of a profile.

Instant messaging

Instant messaging is a way to exchange messages instantly between two or more users. Usually online software is used to make connections between the users and provide an environment where they can chat, share files such as images, and use emoticons.

Client and server roles in instant messaging

The chat program is processed on the user's computer (the CLIENT). Each person chatting holds a local copy on their own computer. Other processing may be carried out on the SERVER, for example when users are logging in.

Worked example

There are advantages and disadvantages to social networking and instant messaging.

Drag and drop the statements into the correct places in the table.
(6 marks)

For drag-and-drop questions, always read all the statements carefully first.

Advantages	Disadvantages
Able to communicate in real time	Viruses could spread
Cheap to use	Needs internet access
Able to do video conferencing/sharing/gaming	May lead to misunderstandings

Now try this

Explain how instant messaging is different from email as a method of communication.   **(2 marks)**

Voice over Internet Protocol

VoIP (Voice over Internet Protocol) is a method of real-time communication over the internet, for example Skype™. The data transmitted is audio and video as two computers are connected through their unique IP addresses.

Advantages of VoIP

- ✓ Able to contact someone anywhere in the world where there is an internet connection
- ✓ Uses internet-only so no additional cost (unlike phone calls)
- ✓ Reduces travel costs, travel time, etc.

Disadvantages of VoIP

- ✗ Relies on internet connection so it can be a slow connection or it can cut out
- ✗ As the audio is being converted to digital, transmitted over the internet and converted back again, the voice quality can be affected
- ✗ Data exchanged over the internet is at risk of security threats such as hackers

A headset like this can be used for VoIP.

Worked example

A business is working with a supplier based in another country.

> Why might they be reluctant to use only VoIP for the weekly meetings? Choose **one** answer from the following options.   **(1 mark)**

A ☐ It is more expensive   B ✓ The quality isn't always reliable

C ☐ They will need to hire a separate venue   D ☐ They want to be able to use video

---

Now try this

VoIP is being used by a business to allow colleagues in different branches to hold weekly meetings.

> Explain **two** benefits to the business of using this technology.   **(4 marks)**

Remember to read the question carefully!

Cloud computing

Cloud storage

Cloud computing is where data is saved on external servers instead of the user's hard drive. The external servers are called HOSTS and are owned by a HOSTING COMPANY. Some well-known examples are Dropbox™, Microsoft–One D™ and Google® Cloud.

Cloud users can access software, data and storage provided by their hosting company.

Users usually access the cloud through a web browser or mobile app – they do not directly access the servers.

Benefits of cloud storage:

☑ COST

You only pay for the storage that you use. You do not have to provide and maintain the hardware.

☑ AVAILABILITY

Data can be available anywhere in the world where there is an internet connection.

Drawbacks of cloud storage:

☒ RELIABILITY

It depends on how reliable the host is to access your data.

☒ SOFTWARE

The company may not be using the latest, fastest version.

☒ SECURITY

You have no control over the files stored and you have to trust the company to keep them safe.

☒ POTENTIAL LOW PERFORMANCE

The speed of accessing data might be slower than using installed software.

Worked example

1 Explain how data is stored in cloud computing. **(2 marks)**

2 Explain how data is stored in installed software. **(2 marks)**

1 In cloud computing, data is saved to external servers (hosts).

2 In installed software, data is saved to the computer's hard drive.

Note how many advantages are asked for, and how many marks are available.

Now try this

Name **two** advantages of cloud computing. **(2 marks)**

Ubiquitous computing

Ubiquitous means 'existing everywhere'. Ubiquitous computing is where processors are embedded into everyday objects.

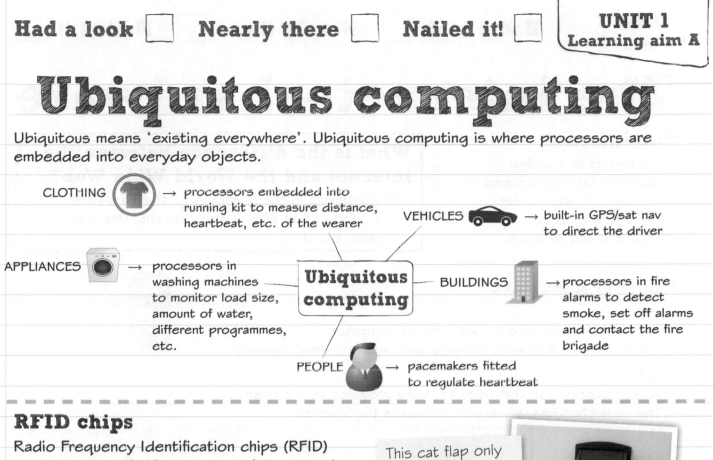

CLOTHING → processors embedded into running kit to measure distance, heartbeat, etc. of the wearer

VEHICLES → built-in GPS/sat nav to direct the driver

APPLIANCES → processors in washing machines to monitor load size, amount of water, different programmes, etc.

Ubiquitous computing

BUILDINGS → processors in fire alarms to detect smoke, set off alarms and contact the fire brigade

PEOPLE → pacemakers fitted to regulate heartbeat

RFID chips

Radio Frequency Identification chips (RFID) are a way to embed processors into everyday objects. They can be used to identify and track an object. It is similar to a bar code, although it does not need to be scanned.

This cat flap only opens for an animal wearing the correct RFID chip.

The Internet of Objects

The Internet of Objects is a concept which looks at the internet as 'things' rather than data. As more objects have processors built-in, this creates a network of physical items. This includes devices, products and even people themselves.

This fridge uses RFID chips to monitor and order groceries.

Worked example

Think carefully about what information the question is asking for.

Describe **one** use of RFID chips in a high street retail shop.
State **one** benefit their introduction could bring.   **(2 marks)**

RFID chips are used for security. There will be scanners near each exit so if a person steals something and tries to take it through an exit without paying the alarms will sound. The benefits of RFID are that items do not need to be scanned like a bar code, they can be scanned just by walking through the sensors.

Now try this

Give **two** examples of where ubiquitous computing might be useful.   **(2 marks)**

The internet – hardware

The internet

The internet is a global network of interconnected computers. It allows data to be exchanged between computers and devices.

> ### What is the difference between the internet and the World Wide Web?
> - The internet is the technology, the hardware.
> - The World Wide Web is the content, the web pages, the data.

Internet hardware

Server
- Runs special software to serve other computers
- Types: file servers, print servers, web servers, email servers

Client
- A computer/device that uses services provided by a server
- The computer/device you use to access the internet is a client

Routers
- Devices which 'route' (direct) traffic (data) through a network
- They are intelligent and will try to find the best routes

Connections/cables
- The connections between this hardware
- Cables, fibre, telephone lines, etc.

Backbone
- A 'big' cable (often fibre) which connects a large number of devices

Server

Backbone

Router

Client   Client   Client

Internet Service Provider

An ISP allows connection to the internet for a client. It would be too expensive to connect directly to the internet so the ISP gives an easy way for connection.

An ISP may provide connection to one client or a network of clients, for example a home network or a business network. ISPs can also provide additional services such as website development and technical support – this is usually for an additional fee.

Worked example

Client	Powerful computer that controls the network
Server	Device which directs traffic over a network
Router	A user's device such as a laptop or smartphone

Match the correct hardware to the definition. **(3 marks)**

Client	A user's device such as a laptop or smartphone
Server	Powerful computer that controls the network
Router	Device which directs traffic over a network

In your online test you can flag a question for review so you can come back to it later.

Now try this

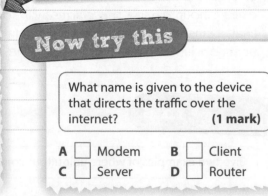

What name is given to the device that directs the traffic over the internet? **(1 mark)**

A ☐ Modem   B ☐ Client
C ☐ Server   D ☐ Router

12

The internet – network diagrams

Network diagrams show how pieces of technology connect together.

This network diagram shows how the key pieces of technology connect together to allow clients to access the internet.

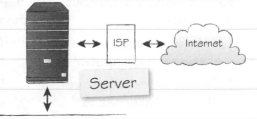

Server

Backbone

Router

Laptop   Computer   Tablet

PoP

Point of Presence (PoP) is an access point to the internet. An ISP may have several PoPs to allow good access to the internet.

NAP

Network Access Point (NAP) is where different networks interconnect, such as your home network onto the internet.

Worked example

This network diagram shows the access points involved in connecting the client so they can access the internet.

Correctly place the terms PoP, NAP and internet in the diagram below.   **(3 marks)**

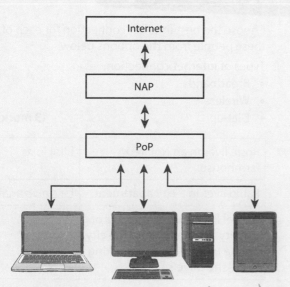

Internet

↕

NAP

↕

PoP

Now try this

Complete this diagram: **(2 marks)**

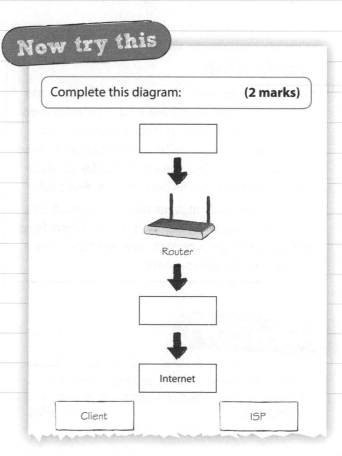

Router

Internet

Client   ISP

Connection methods

There are three methods for connection to the internet. Availability of each may depend on location.

1 Wireless

Connects without using wires

- ✓ Not fixed to a stationary computer
- ✓ Can be used wherever wireless internet is available
- ✗ Needs to have wireless internet available
- ✗ Can be less secure than wired
- ✗ Tends to be slower than wired

2 Broadband

A wired connection through a broadband supplier

- ✓ Better reception and faster than dial-up
- ✗ Wired, so has to be used on a stationary computer

3 Dial-up

A wired connection using a modem and telephone lines

- ✓ Can use existing telephone lines, giving connection where broadband is not available
- ✗ Older technology can give poor reception
- ✗ Conversion between digital and analogue signals can cause errors
- ✗ Usually slower than other methods

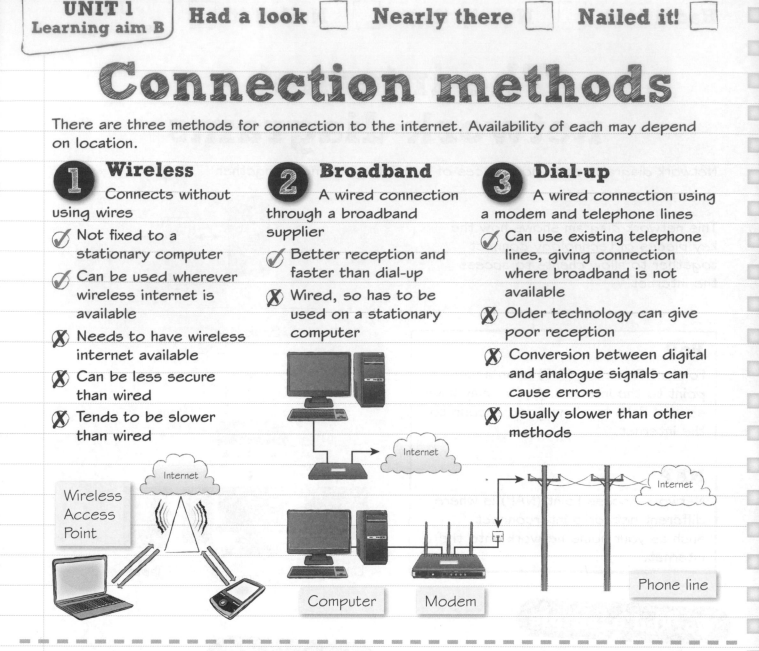

Wireless Access Point

Internet

Computer   Modem

Phone line

Internet

Bandwidth

Bandwidth is how the speed of sections of the internet is measured. It describes how much capacity (space) there is to carry data. Bandwidth is measured in bits per second – the number of bits of data that can be transmitted in one second.

High bandwidth means more information can be moved during that time, therefore giving a faster internet connection and a higher transmission rate.

Remember that broadband is not available in many rural areas.

Worked example

Choose the best internet connection for each of these people from the options below.

Types of internet connection:
- Broadband
- Wireless
- Dial-up   **(3 marks)**

Rosie lives in an isolated farmhouse.	Dial-up
Paulo lives in a city apartment.	Broadband
Rachel lives on the outskirts of the city and travels into the city on the train every day, working while she travels.	Wireless

Now try this

Describe the effect low bandwidth would have on the running of a website and why this might be.   **(2 marks)**

The internet – protocols

Protocols are a set of rules that allow computer systems to connect with different systems to transfer data. This is important on the internet as it involves many different types of devices.

TCP – Transmission Control Protocol

- Takes data from user's application
- Passes it to the Internet Protocol

The reverse happens at the other end of the transmission

IP – Internet Protocol

- Takes data from the Transmission Control Protocol
- Organises it into packets
- Routes it across the network and puts the packets back into the correct order at the other end of the transmission

These two protocols work closely together and are often referred to as TCP/IP

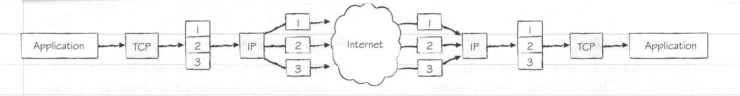

FTP – File Transfer Protocol

FTP is the protocol which allows files to be transferred between two computers or devices. It is usually used to download or upload large files to a server.

A protocol is often called a **handshake** because it is where one computer system connects with a different system to transfer data.

You do not have to give a long answer, but you can make two valid points.

Worked example

Explain the role of a network protocol.
(2 marks)

A protocol is a set of rules to allow communication between different devices on a network.

Now try this

Which **one** of the following is a protocol?
(1 mark)

A ☐ ISP　　B ☐ FTP
C ☐ NAP　　D ☐ HTML

Think about what these letters stand for to answer this question correctly!

World Wide Web

The World Wide Web is the content on the internet. This includes the web pages, files and other data.

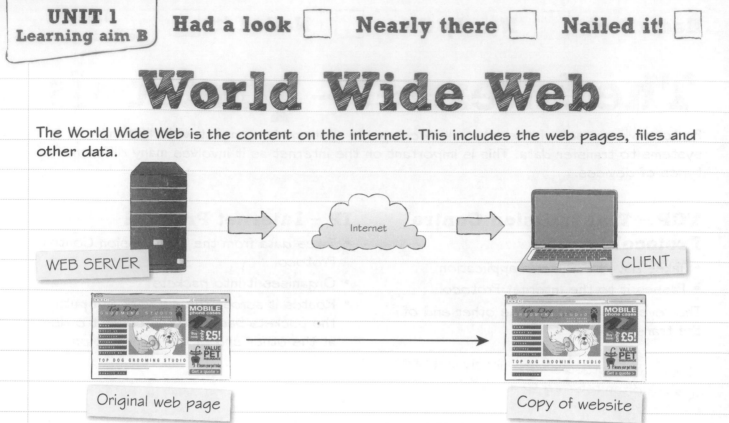

WEB SERVER

Internet

CLIENT

Original web page

Copy of website

Hyperlinks

The World Wide Web works because of hyperlinks. They connect web pages together. When a hyperlink is clicked, a user is taken to another page on a website or a different website.

Web servers

Websites are stored on web servers. When a user accesses a website through a web browser it is temporarily downloaded onto their computer. It is the web server's job to deliver the web page requested.

Browsers

Web pages are accessed through web browsers. These are applications which allow a user to enter a URL and view a web page.

Google UK

| Advanced search
Language tools

Google Search   I'm Feeling Lucky

Advertising Programmes   Business Solutions   +Google   About Google   Google.com

© 2013 - Privacy & Terms

Internet | Protected Mode: Off   100%

Google and the Google logo are registered trademarks of Google Inc., used with permission.

Worked example

Describe what a hyperlink is and what it does.   **(2 marks)**

A hyperlink is text or an image on a web page that can be clicked and then takes the user to another page or file. It allows web pages to be connected together and is the element that creates the World Wide Web.

Now try this

Explain how a user requests a web page and how it then appears on a user's screen.   **(4 marks)**

If a question is asking you to 'explain', make sure that you expand your answer to include all the necessary information.

16

HTML

HTML (HyperText Markup Language) is the language used to create web pages.

HTML tags

HTML is made of up tags. Most of them are in pairs. Pairs of tags are called HTML ELEMENTS.

The open tag is written between triangular brackets < >.

Most tags also have a close tag, which is the same as an open tag but includes a forward slash e.g. <b>text</b>

> You don't need to memorise these tags for your assessment but you should know how to apply them to achieve a certain task.

Some more examples of HTML tags

<b>	bold
<i>	italic
<p>	paragraph
<img>	image
<a href>	hyperlink
<li>	list
<ul>	bullet

An example of HTML

Here is a section of HTML from a web page. The image on the right shows how it would be displayed. See if you can work out what all the tags are for.

```
<html>
<body>
<font size="11"><b>Welcome</b> to my page</font>
<p>I go to <a href="http://www.glenview.ac.uk">
Glen View High School</a></p>
<p><img src="football.jpg">My hobby is football.</p>
</body>
</html>
```

Welcome to my page

I go to Glen View High School

My hobby is football.

> Be very careful as every character will be important!

Now try this

Write the HTML to create a hyperlink to www.penguins.com where the user would click on the image below, called penguins.jpg. **(3 marks)**

Worked example

Write the HTML to create a hyperlink to www.penguins.com where the user would click on the text "Click here to see more penguins". **(2 marks)**

<a href="http://www.penguins.com/">Click here to see more penguins</a>

URLs

A URL (Uniform Resource Locator) is an address for a web page.

A URL is made up of several parts.

Protocols
These tell the browser what to do with the URL

Path
This points to a specific web page

http://www.edexcel.com/subjects/BTEC-IT/

Domain name　This is the name of the website

Web protocols

There are several protocols which are used on web pages. They are included in the URL so that the browser knows how to handle that page.

- HTTP stands for HyperText Transfer Protocol. It is the protocol that allows us to request web pages and download them to our computers.
- FTP stands for File Transfer Protocol.

The URLs for most web pages begin with **http://www**, but web pages that have uploads and downloads usually use **ftp://**.

Worked example

Label the **three** parts of this URL and draw the brackets to show how the URL divides into these three parts.　　**(3 marks)**

Protocol

Path

http://www.edexcel.com/btec/btecfirst/specification.pdf

Domain name

Now try this

Label the **three** parts of this URL　　**(3 marks)**

Make sure you write something different for each of the three parts of the URL.

http://www.pixies.com/magic/

☐☐☐

Search engines

Search engines are websites which allow users to find data on the internet. Examples include google.com and bing.com.

Another name for WEB SPIDERS is WEB CRAWLERS. These are small automated programs (or bots) that automatically carry out these processes all the time without any human involvement.

The user enters keywords into the search engine

The search engine searches its indexed database of web pages on the internet

All the time, web spiders are moving around the internet looking for new web pages. When they find it, they log it in an indexed database

The results are displayed in order of popularity, with sponsored links at the top.

Companies pay money so that links come at the top of the results. These are called SPONSORED LINKS. The more the company pays, the more likely it is to appear in searches. For example, a lower price may have a company's link appear in searches including keywords such as 'pet shop' 'Durham' 'reptiles' 'exotic', which is quite specific. But a higher price may have a company's link appear for every search including the phrase 'pet shop'.

Worked example

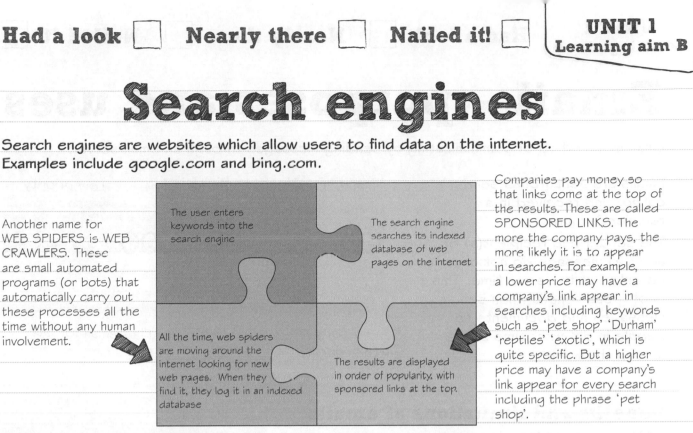

Describe the **three** different types of results in this image. **(3 marks)**

Google and the Google logo are registered trademarks of Google Inc., used with permission.

Sponsored links, which have been paid for, are listed first in the results. Adverts are down the right-hand side and are chosen based on the search key words. The rest of the results are listed in order of popularity.

Now try this

Explain how a search engine works. **(2 marks)**

Make sure you are clear that web spiders search the internet **all the time**. Do not say that they search after the user enters key words.

Email – purposes and uses

Email is a method of communicating by sending messages through an email server.

Emails are sent from a sender's outbox and received in a recipient's inbox.

The sender and recipient(s) of an email message do not have to be online at the same time. This is of great benefit when sending messages and documents to people in different time zones around the world.

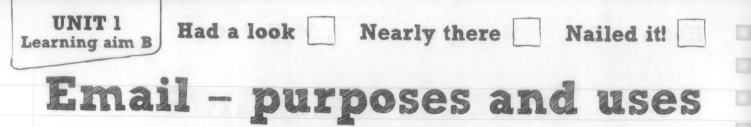

Send   Attach   High priority   Low priority

Send a copy to another person

Address book

Flag email for later

Benefits and limitations of emails

✓ You can send files as attachments
✓ You can send messages to multiple people at the same time
✓ It is faster than post
✓ You can forward messages you have received to other people
✓ You can record contacts in an address book so you can access them quickly
✓ Webmail providers (including Hotmail and Gmail) tend to store emails on a remote provider, meaning that you can access them anywhere via a web browser
✓ You can set up distribution lists to quickly send to multiple people at the same time

✗ Viruses can be spread through emails
✗ Phishing emails may be received (asking for private information)
✗ Employees in a business may spend time on personal email at work
✗ Emails may be intercepted and read by hackers
✗ Spam can be irritating, waste time and take up space in an inbox

Spam is electronic junk mail.

When talking about multiple people, you **must** say 'at the same time'. You could send a letter to multiple people, but not at the same time.

The question says **explain**, so you need to give one advantage, one disadvantage, and write a sentence for each, explaining your reasons.

Worked example

Identify **three** parts of an email which may indicate it is a phishing email.   **(3 marks)**

Strange email address, misspelt word, request for pin number

Now try this

Explain **one** advantage and **one** disadvantage for using email in a business.
(4 marks)

Email – protocols

Email is known as a STORE and FORWARD system.

An email system

POP3, IMAP, and SMTP are all communication protocols used when sending and receiving emails.

SMTP is typically used to send messages from a home computer to a server

POP3 takes the email from the server and delivers it to the recipient's computer

SEND → SENDER'S EMAIL SERVER → RECIPIENT'S EMAIL SERVER → RECIPIENT'S COMPUTER

IMAP keeps the email on the server

Useful facts about email protocols

A protocol allows different software and devices to communicate so you can send an email on a computer and it is received on a phone or tablet.

SMTP	Simple Mail Transfer Protocol	'Push' – pushes the mail from the server to the client
POP3	Post Office Protocol 3	'Pull' – pulls the mail from the server to the client when requested
IMAP	Internet Message Access Protocol	Used for webmail

Worked example

Explain the 'store and forward' system.
(2 marks)

Email is sent by the sender client to the email server. It is 'stored' there until the recipient client requests access and then the email is 'forwarded' to their computer.

Worked example

Select the appropriate word or phrase for each statement.
(3 marks)

IMAP is the email protocol used in *forums / webmail / instant messaging*.

The advantage of this system is that it can be accessed anywhere *where there is an internet connection / in the UK / in the world*.

It relies on the uptime of *the host company / the device manufacturer / the search engine*.

You need to select one answer from the three options in each statement. In the onscreen test this would appear as a drop-down menu.

Now try this

1 Explain the SMTP email protocol. **(2 marks)**
2 Explain the role of the POP3 email protocol. **(2 marks)**

Data exchange – packet switching

Packet switching is the process of data being broken into 'packets' before being sent through a network and then reassembled at the other end. This method is used on the internet.

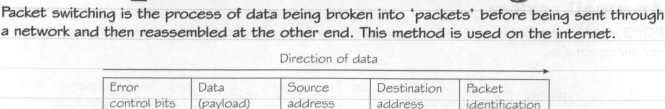

Direction of data

Error control bits	Data (payload)	Source address	Destination address	Packet identification

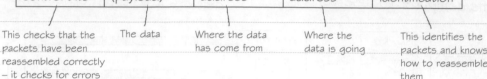

This checks that the packets have been reassembled correctly – it checks for errors

The data

Where the data has come from

Where the data is going

This identifies the packets and knows how to reassemble them

VoIP and packet switching

VoIP uses CODECS at either end to encode and decode data. The sender's computer records a message using a webcam and microphone. The message is converted into digital data, which is then broken into packets to be sent across the internet. The received computer receives the packets, assembles them and decodes the data so it can be seen and heard.

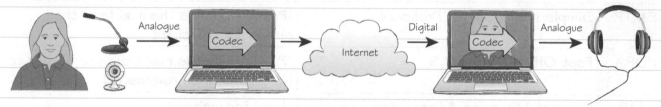

Analogue → Codec → Internet → Digital → Codec → Analogue

Advantages of packet switching

✓ Sends data across a network efficiently.

✓ It means big files which would otherwise clog up the network, can be sent whole.

✓ Allows efficient movement of data through a network because small packets can choose different routes through the network.

✓ There is a security benefit because if a packet is intercepted, the hacker will only have one part of the whole file.

Disadvantages of packet switching

✗ If one or more packets are lost or corrupted during transmission, the whole file will not be received correctly.

Worked example

Explain how packet switching works. **(2 marks)**

Packet switching is used for data sent across a network such as the internet. Data is prepared for transmission by being broken into packets with information such as source and destination and error checking. The packets are sent over the network separately and by different routes. They are then reassembled and checked at the other end.

Now try this

1 Explain **one** advantage of packet switching over the internet. **(2 marks)**

2 Explain **one** disadvantage of packet switching over the internet. **(2 marks)**

Data exchange – transmission modes

Transmission modes are ways in which devices on a network communicate with each other and transmit data.

There are three types of transmission mode.

Transmission modes are used by digital devices such as those shown below.

send → receive

(a) simplex

send → receive
receive ← send

(b) full-duplex

send → ● ← receive
receive ● send

(c) half-duplex

Simplex – signals go in one direction at a time.

Full-duplex – signals go in both directions at the same time.

Half-duplex – signals go in both directions but the devices don't transmit at the same time.

Characteristics of data transmission

Transmission mode	Data transfer	Benefit	Limitation
Serial	Bits of data are transferred one at a time over a wire	Good over large distances	Complex because data has to be broken into individual bits
Parallel	Bits of data are transferred simultaneously over a wire – a whole byte can be transferred at the same time	Faster because more bits are transferred per second	Shorter distance, maximum about 5 metres

Full-Duplex is bi-directional because the signals travel in both directions.

Worked example

Choose a transmission mode for the devices below and explain your choice. The first one has been done for you. **(4 marks)**

Device	Transmission Mode	Explanation
Control system on a production line	Half-duplex	Signals go in both directions to monitor and send instructions. They do not need to go at the same time.
Mouse connecting to a computer	Simplex	Signals go in one direction at a time
Smartphone synching to a computer	Full-duplex	Signals go in both directions at the same time.

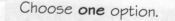

Choose **one** option.

Now try this

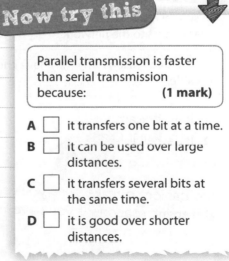

Parallel transmission is faster than serial transmission because: **(1 mark)**

A ☐ it transfers one bit at a time.

B ☐ it can be used over large distances.

C ☐ it transfers several bits at the same time.

D ☐ it is good over shorter distances.

Wired transmission methods

Some devices are connected with wires. There are three transmission methods you need to know about.

UTP/STP

Unshielded twisted pair (UTP) is cable made up of pairs of copper wires twisted together. STP is the same with shielding. Shielded cable has a protective layer around the copper wires (under the plastic coating) to protect the data from interference.

✓ Interference is lessened due to the twisting
✓ Cheaper than other methods
✓ Reliable
✗ Slow
✗ Low capacity
✗ Used over short distances
✗ Susceptible to noise, which means the data can be interfered with if near another digital device or signal

Examples of use: Connecting computers to a network backbone

Coaxial

Solid copper wire with thick shielding.

✓ Reliable
✗ Slow
✗ Low capacity
✗ Used over short distances
✗ Thick and physically inflexible
✗ Susceptible to noise

Examples of use:
TV networks e.g. TV to aerial

Fibre optic

Glass or plastic cables which use light to transmit data

✓ Fast
✓ Used over long distances
✓ Little interference
✗ Expensive
✗ Complex to install (needs a specialist)

Example of use:
Backbone of a network

A school has used STP to connect computers in their classrooms to the network.

> Give **two** reasons why they have chosen this type of cable. **(2 marks)**

1 It is cheap.
2 It is reliable.

It's easier to make sure you've given two **different** reasons if you have numbered them.

> Match up the cable type with its description. **(2 marks)**

Fibre optic	slow, low capacity
UTP	fast, expensive
Coaxial	cheap

In the online test you would have to click on a cable type, then a description to join them with a line.

Wireless transmission methods

Wireless transmission methods do not use cables. Data is transmitted through the air using electromagnetic waves.

① Infrared

Uses infrared light to transfer data (invisible to the human eye)

- ✓ Reliable
- ✗ Short range
- ✗ Devices must be in line of sight
- ✗ Can suffer from interference

Example of use: Television remote, keyboard and mouse connecting to computer

② Microwave

Uses short wavelengths to transmit data (invisible to the human eye)

- ✓ Good for longer distances
- ✗ Can suffer from interference from other devices

Example of use: Bluetooth

③ Satellite

Uses satellites in space to relay data between different points on Earth

- ✓ Good for very long distances
- ✗ Very expensive

Example of use: Global communication systems

Wireless networking

Devices using wireless networking will need a wireless network interface card (NIC). An NIC is the hardware in a device which allows it to receive wireless signals. Although it is called a 'card', it is often built into the device, especially in modern laptops, tablets and smartphones. The NIC will connect to Network Access Points (NAPs). NAPs are points where wireless is distributed, which means a mobile device can pick up the internet. A lot of businesses, such as McDonalds, now have wireless NAPs for their customers.

Worked example

Explain **one** advantage of connecting to the internet wirelessly. **(2 marks)**

Wireless networking means that a user can connect a device to the internet anywhere where there is an internet connection.

It is very important that you say "where there is an internet connection", otherwise it is an unrealistic answer.

Now try this

A small business has used Bluetooth to connect computers to one printer in the office.

| Identify which **two** of these issues might cause problems. **(2 marks)** |

Choose **two** options to get both marks.

A ☐ The printer is a long way away from the computer.

B ☐ The printer is being used by many users at the same time.

C ☐ The printer is near a kitchenette where there is a kettle and a microwave.

D ☐ The printer's NIC is at the back of the device.

E ☐ The printer is plugged into a socket next to the computer.

Client-side processing

Client-side processing uses the client's computer to process web page data in data exchange.

Client-side processing is where the interactivity on a web page is downloaded and processed using the client's processor.

The code which makes this possible is a scripting language (web scripts).

Web scripts are included in the code of the web page and run when the page is loaded into the user's browser. In client-side processing it matters which browser the user is using, because this will affect how the script is understood by the computer and shown on screen.

An example is a rollover image on a web page which changes when a user hovers their mouse over it. This is processed on the client's computer because the web page has downloaded to their machine.

How web pages work

When a client requests a web page, the web server downloads a copy of it onto the client's computer.

Original website on web server   Copy downloaded   Processing occurs on the client

Benefits and drawbacks

☑ Speed – faster because the data is on the client and does not need to move across the internet

☑ Security – data cannot be intercepted on the client in the way it can when it moves across the internet

☒ Browser-specific – different browsers process scripts in different ways, therefore the web page owner cannot be sure how their web page will appear on screen

☒ Computer speed – the web page owner is reliant on the processor speed of the client's computer, so if that is slow then the processing will be slow

Worked example

Identify which **one** of these processes is more likely to occur on the client's processor.
(1 mark)

A ☑ Mini games

B ☐ Login form

C ☐ Paying by credit card

D ☐ Web page

Form data is entered on a web page and then passed back to the web server for processing. A game uses the client's processor to free up space in the web server's processor.

Now try this

Describe **one** reason a web page may use client-side processing for a clock on their website. **(2 marks)**

Remember to think carefully about what information the question is asking you for.

Server-side processing

Server-side processing uses the web server to process web page data.

Server-side processing is where the interactivity on a web page is processed on the web server.

The code which makes this possible is a scripting language (web scripts).

Web scripts are included in the code of the web page and run when the page is loaded into the user's browser. In server-side processing it does not matter which browser the user is using because the processing is done on the web server.

An example is a form completed online which is filled in by the user then submitted to the server where the results are processed and stored.

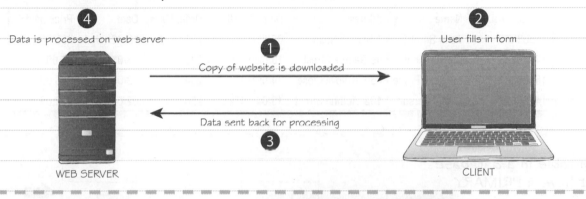

4 Data is processed on web server

1 Copy of website is downloaded →

← Data sent back for processing **3**

WEB SERVER

2 User fills in form

CLIENT

Benefits and drawbacks of server-side processing

- ✓ Efficiency – the information to process does not need to be downloaded to the client's computer
- ✓ Browser independent – it does not matter which browser the user has as the work is done separately on the server
- ✓ Speed – the processing occurs on the web server, which is likely to be more powerful than a client's computer
- ✗ Security – when data is transferred across the internet it is more at risk of security threats
- ✗ Overloading – if a lot of users are asking the web server to process data, it could overload the server and cause it to run slowly or crash

Now try this

(a) Explain what server-side processing is. **(2 marks)**

(b) Describe the benefits and the disadvantages of this type of data exchange. **(4 marks)**

Note how many marks are available and answer all parts of the question.

Database theory

Databases are a vital tool in computing. Most websites are based on databases.

A database is a collection of data.

A set of data is stored in a TABLE, for example information about all of the learners in a school.

A row in a table that stores data about a single item is a RECORD, for example information about one learner.

The columns in a table store categories called FIELDS, for example Name, Address, Gender, Date of Birth.

Customer ID ▾	Name ▾	Address ▾	Date of Birth ▾	Order ID ▾	Date ▾	Price paid ▾
14562375	John Smith	1 Station Road	06/05/1977	231	13/02/2014	£25.00
14678235	Meena Patel	49 George Street	13/02/1949	242	23/01/2014	£6.00
15326342	Michelle Pryce	45 Foxglove Close	14/09/1967	234	03/05/2014	£56.00
14567823	Tom Paterson	103 Victoria Street	13/04/1972	256	02/04/2014	£22.00

Each table in a database must have a PRIMARY KEY. This is a unique piece of data which identifies one record. For example, a Student ID number. To connect tables together, another table should have a FOREIGN KEY. This is the primary key in a different table and creates a RELATIONSHIP.

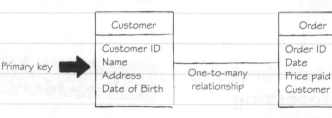
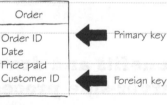

Data types used in databases

Data type	Description	Example
Text	Characters (letters, numbers and symbols)	TVO4 7DG
Number	Numerical value	1.4
Date/time	Dates and times	01/2014
Boolean	Yes/no, also known as true/false	Yes

Databases in practice

Businesses use databases to store huge quantities of data which can be inputted, searched and outputted on screen or printed.

A business database can be local or online.

- A local database is stored and accessed on its own network. This means the data is more protected as data is not moving across the internet. It is only good for a business that is small or willing to pay for networking between different branches of their business.

- An online database uses the internet to share access to it from locations all around the world. It can be accessed 'on the move' through wireless internet where there is an internet connection. The data is still usually only available through logging in, but security is more difficult.

Google and the Google logo are registered trademarks of Google Inc., used with permission.

Social media, such as Facebook, retail sites, such as Amazon, and search engines, such as Google, are all run on databases.

Facebook uses a database to store users' profiles and all of their data.

Google

Search engines use databases to store information which is searched when the user enters key words.

Database Management Systems (DBMS)

This is software that allows you to create and use your own databases. It creates tables and fields, and can sort and search for data. It can also allow for different levels of access by different users.

Structured Query Language (SQL)

This is the language that can be used to create databases. It is made up of two parts:
- Data Definition Language (DDL) – defines the structure of the database
- Data Manipulation Language (DML) – can make changes such as add, delete and change – also creates queries

Worked example

Select **two** reasons why a company might use a database.   **(2 marks)**

A ☑ Easy to search for specific records
B ☐ Only one user can access the data at a time
C ☐ Easy to add new records, although difficult to edit them
D ☑ More secure than paper records
E ☐ Records can be deleted easily

Now try this

(a) State **one** feature of a local database.
(b) State **one** feature of an online database.

Remember to think carefully about what information the question is asking you for.

Threats to data

Threats are risks to the security of data or equipment.

Opportunity threats

Threats from people who see an opportunity, such as an unattended computer.

Computer viruses

Malicious programs that try to replicate and spread across a computer or a network.

Other malware

This includes Trojans, worms, adware, spyware and other nasty software that is aiming to cause damage or steal data.

Phishing

A fake email or website that is trying to trick the user into handing over their personal data.

A high proportion of hackers are internal to the organisation.

Accidental damage

This could include floods, fire or hurricanes, or damage from untrained users.

Hackers

People who purposefully try to gain unauthorised access.

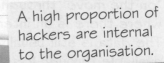

Worked example

> Complete this text to show why security is important.   **(3 marks)**

A business does not have adequate security.

- There is a risk that information might be stolen. This information is known as | intellectual property |.
- Competitors may use this to create their own inferior version of a product.
- This could lead to mistrust.
- This may damage the company's | reputation |.
- Ultimately this could lead to loss of | profits |.

Now try this

> Describe **two** threats which can affect a business' data.   **(4 marks)**

Describe means you have to name the threats and explain what they are.

Protection of data

Physical barriers

Real world protection such as locks on doors, CCTV cameras and turning computers off at night.

Password control of access

Using strong passwords that are at least eight characters long and include at least one uppercase letter, lowercase letter, number and symbol.

Access levels

Ensuring people only have access to the parts of the system they need and training them before giving them greater access (more information on page 6).

Anti-virus software

Software that deletes or quarantines viruses.

> Be careful not to call it virus software.

Firewall

Software that monitors data coming in and out of a network and protects it from viruses, malware and hackers. It puts a 'wall' around a network.

Encryption

Turning data into a secret code before sending it over a network or the internet, so that if it is intercepted it will not be understood.

Backup and recovery

Making a copy of data in a different place to the original data in case the original becomes corrupt or is accidentally deleted.

Identity theft

Identity theft is where someone uses another individual's personal details to pretend they are them. They may set up accounts, access bank accounts or make purchases. This threat can be prevented most effectively by users keeping their personal details private, including on social networking sites.

Recovery

Replacing the data if something happens, such as deletion or corruption. This may include copying the files from the backup to their original location or using a software recovery tool. In servers, this may involve replacing a damaged drive with a new one already loaded with the backup data.

Personal safety

Security settings can be used on social networking sites to protect users' privacy and reputation.

This is important as not everyone is who they claim to be. Also, you might not want your teacher or colleague to see something that is embarrassing or harmful to your reputation.

Now try this

Explain **two** measures you can take to protect your e-reputation.   **(4 marks)**

> The question is worth four marks – you need to give a detailed explanation of data protection measures to get full marks.

Legislation

You should know the basics of some UK legislation.

Data Protection Act 1998

Businesses must conform to the eight principles to protect the data that they hold about customers.

Computer Misuse Act 1990

This law was created to punish hackers and creators of viruses.

Copyright, Designs and Patents Act 1988

Copyright protects people's original data such as artworks, music, code, books, etc.

Freedom of Information Act 2000

This gives people the right to see data held about them by organisations, and also to request access to data about organisations such as local councils or national government.

Technology used for monitoring

Technology can be used to monitor people's movements and communications.

Movements:
- CCTV cameras
- GPS devices (like those in smartphones)
- Data from airports, such as passenger lists

Communications:
- Monitoring email
- Monitoring website visits
- Logging keywords typed into search engines

Worked example

Carla uses a social media website and has started chatting regularly to a user called Brian. It looks like they have a lot in common and he has sent her photographs of himself. He has recently suggested that they meet for a coffee, as they live quite close to each other.

> Describe the **two** potential risks of this situation and describe what Carla should do. **(6 marks)**

Carla does not know Brian personally, therefore she cannot trust what he says or know that the photos are actually of him. She should not meet him at his home as it could be dangerous. If she chooses to meet him, then she should not go alone, should make sure other people know where she will be and only agree to meet him somewhere public, such as a café.

Now try this

Sam is setting up a new café as a business. He uses a search engine to find images from UK websites and adds them to his menu.

> Select **two** statements that are true about this situation by ticking the boxes below. **(2 marks)**

A ☐ All images on the internet are free from copyright so can be used wherever he wants.

B ☐ He has broken UK law because he is making money from his café.

C ☐ He has not broken the law because he did not know the images were protected under copyright.

D ☐ He is likely to be fined under the Copyright, Designs and Patents Act 1988.

E ☐ He has not broken the law because his images are not from a company website.

Exam skills 1

The onscreen test for Unit I lasts one hour and includes a variety of question types. There will be questions on ALL the learning aims: A, B and C. You can answer the questions in any order.

Practise

☑ The more you revise the more you will understand.

☑ Complete as many practice questions as you can prior to the test.

☑ Practise all of the different types of question.

☑ Practise marking questions too – it will help you to see what the question is asking.

Answering multiple-choice questions

☑ Read the question carefully.

☑ Look out for the KEY WORDS in the question.

☑ Read all the options carefully.

☑ Rule out any answers that you know are wrong.

☑ Read the CONTEXT of the question – look for the most appropriate answer.

☑ Select the most appropriate answer for the context.

You can navigate forwards and backwards through your online test. This means you can check your answers and change them if necessary before submitting your test.

Worked example

> Which **one** of the following is a real-time online service? **(1 mark)**
>
> Click on **one** of the boxes.
>
> A ☐ Retail website   B ☑ Pollen count website
>
> C ☐ Museum website   D ☐ Astronomy website

You only need to click on **one** of the boxes. If you click a second box the online test will **change** your answer.

Worked example

> Select the correct explanation for these **two** terms.   **(2 marks)**
>
> *Blog*   A website whose purpose is for users to communicate with each other
>
>   A regular downloadable audio file
>
>   An online journal
>
> *Podcast*   An app where very short messages can be sent and received

To answer this question, you would click on the term on the left then on the answer on the right – a line will appear connecting them.

> Label the **three** parts of this URL.   **(6 marks)**
>
> http://www.lancashiremuseums.co.uk/visit/january/
>
> protocol   domain name   path

Other possibilities for this type of question might include drag-and-drop from a selection of terms into blank boxes.

Exam skills 2

It is important to familiarise yourself with the features of the online test.

TIME: this shows/hides the time that has elapsed since the start of the test. Find it at the bottom right of your screen.

HELP: this tells you about the features of the test and the tools available. It does not provide technical help. If you have a technical problem in the online test then tell the invigilator straight away.

ACCESSIBILITY PANEL: if you are struggling to read the screen, try adjusting the colours or magnifying the screen.

NEXT: this moves the test on to the next question.

WORKING BOX: use the working box for rough notes or calculations at any time.

CALCULATOR: use this when you have to carry out any calculations.

FLAG: you can do the questions in any order. If one puzzles you, leave it and carry on. Use the Flag button to mark it, so you won't forget about it.

REVIEW: this button lets you go back through the test and check your answers. Any questions you 'flagged' show on this screen.

PREVIOUS: this moves the test back to the previous question.

QUIT: when you click this button a pop-up window asks if you want to quit the test. Answer 'yes' or 'no'. If you press 'no' you return to the question you were answering. When you have finished and checked all your answers use this button.

Answering short-answer questions

Some questions will require you to write shorter answers to show your understanding. Most short-answer questions will be worth 1, 2 or 3 marks each.

✓ Read the question carefully.

✓ Look out for the key words.

✓ Look at the number of marks available for the question.

✓ Make sure you make the same number of statements as there are marks available. For example, if the question is worth 3 marks, make at least three statements.

✓ Try not to repeat the question in your answer.

✓ If the question relates to a particular activity then make sure you make reference to it in your answer.

✓ Make sure you look at the key command word – have you been asked to describe, explain or discuss?

Worked example

1 Explain how data is stored in cloud computing. **(2 marks)**

2 Explain how data is stored in installed software. **(2 marks)**

1 In cloud computing, data is saved to external servers (hosts).

2 In installed software, data is saved to the computer's hard drive.

Worked example

Explain **one** advantage of connecting to the internet wirelessly. **(2 marks)**

Wireless networking means that a user can connect a device to the internet anywhere where there is an internet connection.

It is very important that you say "where there is an internet connection", otherwise it is an unrealistic answer.

Exam skills 3

Learn how to spot the different COMMAND words used in questions. Command words tell you exactly what sort of answer is needed.

Key command words

Describe: give a description of...

State: list or name what the question is asking for.

Outline: briefly list the main features.

Identify: select one option or name something.

Explain: give reasons why something is as it is.

Justify: provide reasons why something is valid or why you chose something.

Compare: identify and explain the similarities and differences.

Discuss: give reasons or present facts and explain their impact on the topic.

Summarise: give an account of the main points.

Interpret: make a judgement about something.

What order will you choose?

Look through the questions at the beginning of the test. You can then make a decision about which order you want to answer them in.

Options:

I am going to answer the questions I find easier first then return to the questions that are trickier.

I am going to start at question 1a and continue in sequence to the end.

I am going to start with the longer questions first.

Preparation

It is really important that you prepare well for your test, both in the weeks and days before.

Pace yourself

✓ Think about how you learn best – mind maps, tape recordings, posters, etc. Create materials that will suit you.

✓ Don't leave revision too late – plan well in advance.

✓ Try to find a time and a place where you work best – try to avoid distractions.

✓ Make sure you're you are organised. Keep all your revision notes in order.

Checklist for the day

✓ Get up in plenty of time – don't be rushed.

✓ Eat well.

✓ Get there early.

✓ Make sure you know how long you have in the test.

✓ Work out how long you can spend on each question.

✓ Check the spelling in your answers.

Technology systems

A computer is a machine that processes digital data.

A computer installation is made up of a collection of components to form a technology system.

Technology is an essential component of industry and services. Here is what technology is used for in the construction, finance, health, retail and manufacturing sectors.

Manufacturing sector

Use technology for Computer Aided Design (CAD) and Computer Aided Manufacture (CAM). These are technology systems used to design component parts on a computer. The designs are then sent to robotic systems that manufacture the parts.

Construction sector

Building houses, factories, bridges and large buildings; architecture.

Use technology to:
- plan projects
- create architecture drawings
- track spending on a project
- create simulations (to test a structure before building it)

Health sector

Doctors, hospitals, pharmacies and other medical organisations.

Use technology to:
- scan patients (e.g. MRI, x-ray)
- monitor heart beats, breathing, etc. on life support machines
- store patient records digitally

Retail sector

Selling products to customers.

Use technology to:
- track sales using tills at PoS (Point of Sale)
- advertise online and use e-commerce to sell products
- produce reports about sales and profits

Finance sector

Involving money – mostly banking.

Use technology to:
- follow prices of stocks and shares
- calculate interest rates on loans and savings
- internet banking for customers

Worked example

Match these sectors and their uses of technology.   **(4 marks)**

Finance ───────── Robots on a production line

Manufacturing ─── Point of Sale tills

Health ────────── Calculating the interest on a loan

Retail ────────── Digital patient records

Now try this

Give **two** examples to explain how the construction sector uses technology. **(4 marks)**

The question asks for **two** examples but is worth four marks – so make sure to give explanations for each example.

Issues in technology systems

Technology systems can have both positive and negative impacts on the environment. Here are some examples.

Environment

How technology systems are environmentally friendly:

- ✓ Create sustainability. For example, video conferencing reduces the need to travel.
- ✓ Emails can send documents electronically, which reduces the use of paper and space needed to store it.
- ✓ Digitization of things such as books and maps means that less energy is being used to produce physical products.
- ✓ Technology systems, including sensors, analyse data from products such as cars and kettles to enable manufacturers to design more sustainable products.

Sustainability is about protecting the planet and making sure there are resources for the future.

How technology systems are environmentally unfriendly:

- ✗ Bad for the planet – e.g. using electricity, especially if computers are left turned on overnight unused
- ✗ Manufacturing computers use natural resources and electricity.
- ✗ Disposing of old computers creates landfill and can release dangerous chemicals.
- ✗ Computers produce waste heat which then needs electricity to cool, e.g. air conditioning in server rooms needs to be running constantly.

Electricity →   ← Waste heat

Computers use electricity and produce waste heat, particularly if they are left turned on and unused overnight.

Computer security

Threats include: hackers, viruses and other malware.

Prevention methods include: anti-viruses, firewalls, strong passwords and levels of access.

Security is important for personal and sensitive information, such as medical records, personal emails or financial information.

Copyright

Copyright legally protects ownership of data. There is a huge amount of information on the internet and it is a user's responsibility not to breach copyright law.

Copyright means that the person who created the information owns it, and other people cannot use it or claim it as their own. For example, someone who writes a song owns that song, so they can be paid when it is played and can sue if someone else pretends they wrote it.

Worked example

Complete these statements about copyright.
(2 marks)

Images on the internet are protected under copyright. In the UK, the law which protects copyright is the Copyright, Designs and Patents Act 1988 . If someone breaks the law they can be punished by a fine or imprisonment .

Now try this

Describe the effects on the environment of online shopping. **(2 marks)**

Developing technology systems

Technology systems are continually being improved. There are three main reasons why this is important to organisations.

1 Competitive advantage

By developing technology systems, an organisation can create an advantage over a competitor by, for example, making products better or faster, or making use of internet technology.

Example: A car manufacturer may use robots on a production line to create cars, which allow them to mass produce more cars faster. Other manufacturers' cars are hand-assembled, which means they cannot produce as many in the same time.

A business using an automated system may gain competitive advantage over other, more traditional, businesses

2 Reduced costs

Improving technology can make a process in a business cheaper. This can mean lower operating costs (the amount it costs to run the business) and higher profits.

Self-checkouts in a supermarket reduce the number of checkout staff needed, saving the supermarket money

Worked example

Match the **two** reasons for developing technology with **two** examples.   **(2 marks)**

Competitive advantage

Reduced costs

Spending less on raw materials

Finding more competitors

Providing a better service than a similar company

Lowering profit and revenue

3 Improved performance

Developing technology can improve the performance of the business so it can function more efficiently. Efficiency means that processes are faster and tasks can be made easier; staff may be happier and have better job satisfaction.

Now try this

A business that designs and manufactures milk containers and packaging for other dairy products is considering developing its technology systems.

Explain **two** advantages to the business of doing this.   **(4 marks)**

The question asks for **two** advantages but is worth four marks. Therefore an example for each advantage could gain the full marks.

Hardware devices

Devices are items of technology that perform a specific purpose.

Device	Purpose	Example
PC (Personal Computer)	Multi-purpose computer that runs functional software such as word processing and spreadsheets. PC includes Windows, Apple and Linux machines	
Server	A powerful computer that controls other devices on a network.	
Laptop	A mobile (portable) computer.	
Tablet	A mobile device, usually with a touchscreen, about the size of a clipboard.	
Smartphone	A mobile device with a main function of making calls and sending texts but with additional functionality.	
Games console	A device designed primarily for playing games.	
Programmable digital devices	Any object with a digital control.	

Worked example

Aled wants to purchase a device. He mostly wants to be able to surf the web but also needs to access his files to work on them, and use it at work and at home.

(a) Select an appropriate device for him from the list below. **(1 mark)**

A ☐ PC
B ☐ Smartphone
C ☑ Tablet

When a scenario is given, you should use it in your answer.

Explain means you should give a reason and justify it.

(b) Explain why your chosen device is suitable for Aled. **(2 marks)**

Aled should buy a tablet because it is mainly for surfing the web, is mobile so he can use it at home and at work, and he can also access his files if he saves them to the cloud.

Now try this

Using examples, describe what is meant by the term 'programmable digital device' and the purpose of these types of devices. **(4 marks)**

Input and output

Input puts data into a device. Output sends data out of a device.

Input

Keyboard	Mouse

Sensors	Touch screen
Microphone	Scanner
Digital camera/webcam	Game controller

A touch screen can be input and output, because the 'touch' control is input whereas the 'screen' display is output.

Output

Printers	Speakers
Headphones	Screen (monitor)
Projector	Robot/robot arm
Actuator	Force feedback (e.g. vibration in a game controller)

Any technology which connects to a device to expand its functionality is called a **peripheral**.

Worked example

Trevor is creating a podcast. Choose **two** appropriate input and output devices he should use from those shown opposite. **(2 marks)**

Input = microphone
Output = speakers

Now try this

Which **one** of these is an input device? **(1 mark)**

A ☐ Projector   B ☐ Speakers
C ☐ Microphone   D ☐ Headphones

Storage

Storage is a type of memory which holds data. For more on memory and storage, see page 50.

Storage

Magnetic storage media	HDD (Hard Disk Drive)	e.g. hard drive in a PC – can be internal or external	
Solid state media	SSD (Solid State Drive)	e.g. hard drive in a PC – can be internal or external	
	SD cards	e.g. a memory card in a digital camera	
	USB memory stick	Portable storage device	
Optical media	CD	Has a fixed storage size approx. 700Mb	
	DVD	Has a fixed storage size approx. 5–10Gb	

CD and DVD usually refer to disks that already have data written to them and the data is fixed. CD-R and DVD-R disks are blank but can be written once by a user. CD-RW and DVD-RW ('read write') can be written and re-written by the user as many times as needed.

Important note: 'USB' is not a type of storage! USB is the name of the connection. You must use a full name such as USB memory stick. There are two words for it – make sure you use a commonly used name to describe it such as USB pen drive, USB memory stick, USB flash drive, USB thumb drive.

Worked example

Match each device with a suitable storage media. **(3 marks)**

Digital camera ⟶ DVD

Optical media drive in a games console ⟶ Hard disk drive

File storage in a server ⟶ SD card

Now try this

Sadia uses a USB memory stick to save her coursework.

(a) Explain **one** advantage of using this type of storage. **(2 marks)**

(b) Explain **one** disadvantage of using this type of storage. **(2 marks)**

Automated systems

An automated system is a combination of hardware and software to carry out a function without human intervention. Automated systems are usually used to improve productivity and efficiency.

Examples of automated systems

Central heating system in a house

Production lines use robots to carry out repetitive and dangerous tasks.

Robots vs humans

There are some tasks that robots can perform better than humans, and there are some that humans can do better than robots.

Robots are automated and can work without human involvement.

Advantages of robots carrying out tasks	Advantages of humans carrying out tasks
More accurate/can work at smaller detail	Have emotions and empathy (e.g. for working in healthcare or childcare)
Can perform impossible tasks for humans e.g. go to different planets, lift heavier weights	Better movement for walking and running
Able to work in dangerous or unpleasant conditions	Intuitive e.g. for driving
Can perform repetitive tasks without getting bored or tired	Make subjective decisions
Smaller margin of error – can make identical products over and over again perfectly	Adaptable – if a human encounters an error, they can change, whereas a robot will keep repeating the error

Worked example

An automated vacuum cleaner can move around a house, cleaning the carpets and avoiding walls and furniture.

> Explain how input devices and software allow it to 'know' how to move around the house. **(4 marks)**

The automated vacuum cleaner has sensors on it to detect when it is near an object like a chair or a wall. The software will identify it as an obstacle and turn the vacuum cleaner in another direction.

Now try this

(a) Identify **one** input device on this automated system. **(1 mark)**

(b) Identify **one** output device on this system. **(1 mark)**

Devices to capture data

There are some specialist input technologies which capture data for automated systems. Here are five examples.

1 Magnetic strip reader

Magnetic strip readers will read the strip on a card, such as a credit card. The strip is known as a magstripe.

A magstripe.

CARD
1234 5678 9012 3456

2 Optical Character Reader (OCR)

OCR will read characters (text) and convert them into digital text. Simple OCR will convert printed text into digital text. More sophisticated OCR can read handwriting and convert it into digital text.

An OCR reader

3 Optical Mark Reader (OMR)

OMR will read marks on a pre-printed sheet. It is used for surveys, multiple choice forms and lottery tickets.

An OMR sheet

4 Radio Frequency Identification Systems (RFID)

An RFID tag attached to clothing triggers an alarm when passed through scanners near the exits of shops

An RFID tag

5 Barcode scanner

When the barcodes on products in a supermarket are scanned, the unique pattern is turned into a product code which is found in their database of products.

Worked example

Match the data capture methods with a reason for use. **(2 marks)**

OMR

OCR

- Can reduce errors because the user has to choose options available
- Scans a pattern that represents a unique code to identify a product
- Can be scanned at a distance
- Creates a digital file that can be backed up to keep safe

Now try this

Sheppard Airways use a self-check-in machine to make it quicker for passengers to check in for a flight.

Describe the technology this automated system might use. **(2 marks)**

Use the scenario to think about your answer and what the system is required to do.

Types and uses of networks

A network describes computers which have been connected together. Here are four examples.

Types of network

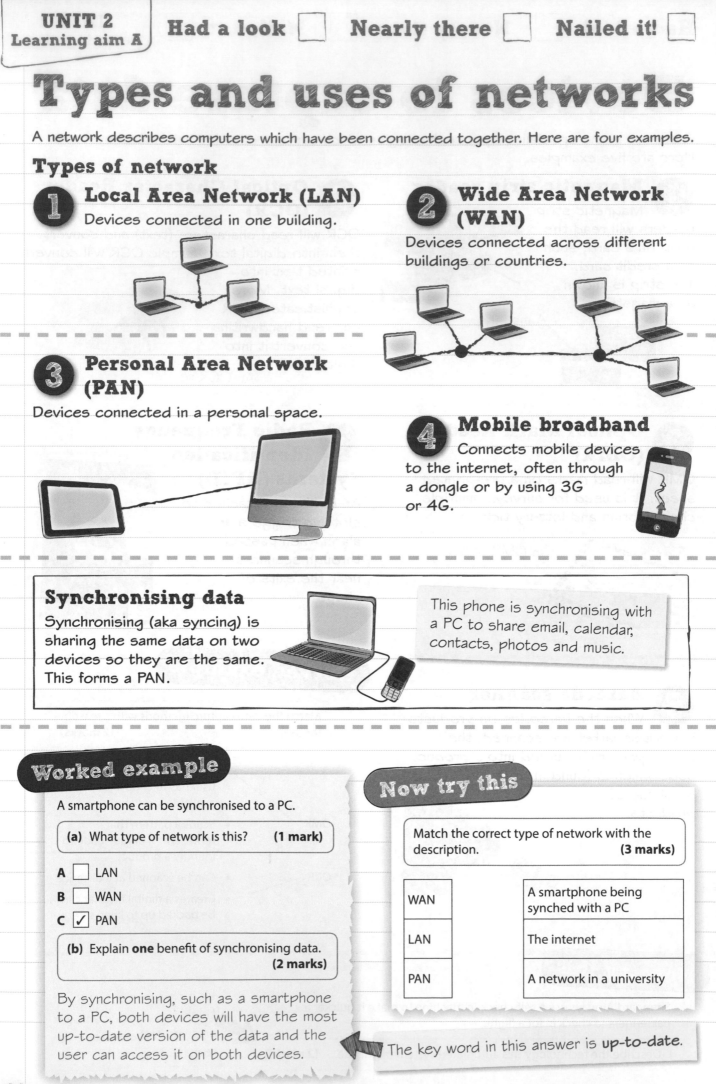

1 Local Area Network (LAN)
Devices connected in one building.

2 Wide Area Network (WAN)
Devices connected across different buildings or countries.

3 Personal Area Network (PAN)
Devices connected in a personal space.

4 Mobile broadband
Connects mobile devices to the internet, often through a dongle or by using 3G or 4G.

Synchronising data
Synchronising (aka syncing) is sharing the same data on two devices so they are the same. This forms a PAN.

This phone is synchronising with a PC to share email, calendar, contacts, photos and music.

Worked example

A smartphone can be synchronised to a PC.

(a) What type of network is this?   **(1 mark)**

A ☐ LAN

B ☐ WAN

C ✓ PAN

(b) Explain **one** benefit of synchronising data.   **(2 marks)**

By synchronising, such as a smartphone to a PC, both devices will have the most up-to-date version of the data and the user can access it on both devices.

Now try this

Match the correct type of network with the description.   **(3 marks)**

WAN	A smartphone being synched with a PC
LAN	The internet
PAN	A network in a university

The key word in this answer is **up-to-date**.

Benefits of networks

Computer networking can have different types of benefits.

Uses of network systems

Common uses of networks		Examples
Sharing	Sharing resources and data with users who have authorised access.	A shared printer in an office, rather than buying one printer for each computer in the office.
Entertainment	Streaming films, listening to radio stations live, joining online gaming communities, social media.	On demand television services allow users to watch programmes that have already been shown on broadcast television.
Communication	Email, instant messaging, video conferencing.	Video conferencing can be used to hold a face-to-face meeting with people in different countries without needing to travel.

Benefits of networking computers

- Sharing resources SAVES MONEY

- Employees can ACCESS files from work or home

- Better communication IMPROVES EFFICIENCY

- Can reduce the need for travel, SAVING TIME and REDUCING POLLUTION

Worked example

A network allows users to share resources.

Select **two** devices that can be shared.
(2 marks)

Think about your classroom – what resources do you share in there?

A ☑ Printer

B ☐ Speakers

C ☐ Keyboard

D ☑ Scanner

Now try this

(a) Name **two** resources that could be shared on an office network.   **(2 marks)**

(b) Describe **one** benefit of each.   **(4 marks)**

Methods of transferring data

A network has to be connected together by physical and/or wireless methods so the data can move around it.

Physical methods

Type	Description	Benefits and drawbacks	Uses
UTP/STP	Unshielded Twisted Pair is pairs of copper wires twisted together. STP is the same with shielding.	• Interference is lessened due to the twisting • Cheaper than other methods • Poor at very high speeds	To connect PCs and printers to a LAN
Fibre optic	Glass or plastic cables which use light to transmit data	• Fast • Used over long distances • Little interference • Expensive	Backbone in a network, to connect between routers and switches
Coaxial	Solid copper wire with thick shielding.	• Reliable • Good for short distances • Slow	Used in older networks and home optical broadband systems

See page 24 for more examples.

Wireless methods

Type	Description	Uses
Wi-Fi	A common technology for wireless networking. In standard build of most modern devices. Needs a Wireless Access Point (WAP) to connect to.	Connecting mobile devices to networks
Bluetooth	Short-range, fairly slow wireless connection	Headsets, wireless keyboards and mice, synchronising between devices

Use the scenario to think about your answer and what is required. Give full explanations to gain the maximum number of marks.

Worked example

Match the physical network methods with their characteristics. **(3 marks)**

UTP —————— Slowest

Fibre optic ——×—— Susceptible to interference

Coaxial ———— Most expensive

Now try this

Jack owns a small business and has just bought new office premises for himself and his four members of staff. He wants to set up a LAN.

Discuss possible connection methods Jack could use for his office. **(8 marks)**

Main components of a computer

Components are the parts inside a device.

> You should be familiar with the components inside a PC – components inside other devices are similar.

Component	Name	Description
	Motherboard	• Allows communication between components • Is a PCB (Printed Circuit Board) where all the other system components plug in
	HDD (Hard Disk Drive) (storage device)	• Permanent memory for data storage See page 50 for more on memory
	RAM (Random Access Memory)	• Temporary memory • Makes processing more efficient See page 50 for more on memory
	PSU (Power Supply Unit)	• Takes power from mains and feeds into motherboard • Fan keeps it cool
	CPU (Central Processor Unit) + fan + heat sink	• Processes data • Fan and heat sink keep it cool See page 48 for inside the CPU
	Graphics card (expansion card)	• Boosts graphics capabilities of those built into motherboard
	Sound card (expansion card)	• Boosts sound capabilities of those built into motherboard.
	Optical drive	• Reads CDs and/or DVDs

Worked example

(a) Which **one** of these components uses a fan to keep them cool? **(1 mark)**

A ☐ Hard drive   B ☐ RAM

C ☑ PSU   D ☐ Motherboard

(b) A CPU uses a fan for cooling.

What cooling method is used on most CPUs in addition to a fan? **(1 mark)**

Heat sink

Now try this

Which **one** of these components is a type of memory? **(1 mark)**

A ☐ CPU   B ☐ RAM   C ☐ PSU   D ☐ Motherboard

> Think about what the initials stand for to help you answer this question!

Processing digital data 1

Inside the CPU there are components that allow it to process instructions.

CPU (Central Processing Unit)

- Each computer has at least one
- Runs instructions (code) in computer programs
- Controls input and output

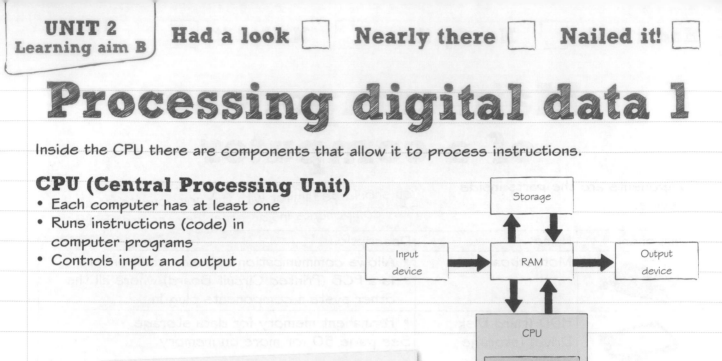

The Central Processing Unit passes data directly back and forth from the RAM. The RAM then transfers data to and from the storage and to the output device.

GPU (Graphical Processing Unit)

A GPU (Graphical Processing Unit) focuses on processing visual data. If a device has a GPU, it frees up the CPU to deal with other types of data.

A GPU is usually on a graphics card and processes graphical data only.

Components inside the CPU

ALU	(Arithmetic and Logic Unit) Carries out calculations and comparisons (used in sorting and searching)
Registers	Store bytes of data which are used by the ALU Also stores the address in RAM so the CPU knows where the next instruction will come from
Control unit	Controls instructions being passed between RAM, registers and the ALU Sends the result of the instructions to the other components

Worked example

What do these terms stand for?   (2 marks)

CPU	Central Processing Unit
GPU	Graphical Processing Unit

In the onscreen test this would be a drag-and-drop question.

Now try this

Match the CPU components with the functions they perform.   (3 marks)

ALU — Passes data to the RAM and other components

Registers — Does comparisons and calculations with bits of data

Control unit — Stores bytes of data that are used by the ALU and the results

Processing digital data 2

The features of the CPU and GPU can affect performance and user experience. Performance is how fast data is processed. User experience is the speed at which the device appears to run to the user. A slow device can be very frustrating to a user!

Here are four factors that affect performance.

① Clock speed

The clock speed determines the speed of the processor.

One clock cycle will process one word of data (see page 54 for more on words)

The clock speed is measured in MHz or GHz.

> **How does this affect performance?**
> Faster clock speed = more instructions processed per second = faster processing.

② Multiple processing cores

Processors often have multiple cores. Each core can process simultaneously.

> **How does this affect performance?**
> More cores = more instructions processed simultaneously per second = faster processing.

③ Cache memory

Cache memory is used between faster and slower devices to let them work more quickly together.

For example, the processor has a cache memory to help speed up access to the slower RAM.

> **How does this affect performance?**
> It buffers the data to feed into the slower device and frees up the faster device for the next process.

④ Data buses

A data bus is a circuit which connects one part of the motherboard to another. The more data it can handle, the faster information can travel between components and the better the performance of the computer.

> **How does this affect performance?**
> More data buses = computer runs faster

Worked example

Penny is choosing a new computer and has narrowed her choice to two devices with these CPU specifications:

PC 1	PC 2
Quad core 2.5GHz	Dual core 2.75GHz

Complete these statements. **(3 marks)**

PC _1_ has more cores and can process more data simultaneously.

PC _2_ can process more words per second.

The CPU that will appear to process the fastest is PC _1_.

> PC 1 has four cores. PC 2 has two cores. Although PC 2 is faster per core, PC 1 has more cores that are still at a good speed.

Now try this

Explain why, in a PC, cache memory might be used between fast RAM and a slow HDD. **(2 marks)**

Memory and storage

Memory is used inside a device for holding data during operation. Storage is used for holding data permanently after the device is turned off so it can be loaded and used later.

Type of memory	Permanent or Temporary	Memory or Storage	Location	Description
ROM (Read Only Memory)	Permanent	Memory	On motherboard	Holds essential data used in boot-up including boot sequence, date and time
RAM (DRAM) (Dynamic Random Access Memory)	Temporary	Memory	Slotted into motherboard	Holds data while the processor is working
HDD (Hard Disk Drive)	Permanent	Storage	Connected to motherboard or external through USB	Uses magnetic disk where binary data is stored as positive or negative + read/write head
SSD (Solid State Drive)	Permanent	Storage	Connected to motherboard or external	Uses FLASH MEMORY with transistors which 'remember' by being turned on or turned off to represent binary
Optical (CDs, DVDs)	Permanent	Storage	Drives at front of case or external	Data is 'burnt' to CDs/DVDs as a pattern of dots to represent binary, which can be read by a light beam such as a laser

Temporary vs permanent

Memory, such as RAM (DRAM) in PCs and laptops, is temporary because the data that is stored is deleted when the device is turned off. Storage, such as HDD and SSD, is permanent because when the device is turned off the data remains saved.

SRAM vs DRAM

DRAM is Dynamic RAM and is used in PCs and laptops.

SRAM is Static RAM (aka Flash Memory) and is used in mobile devices such as smartphones, digital cameras and tablets.

Worked example

Match **each** storage component with **two** characteristics. **(4 marks)**

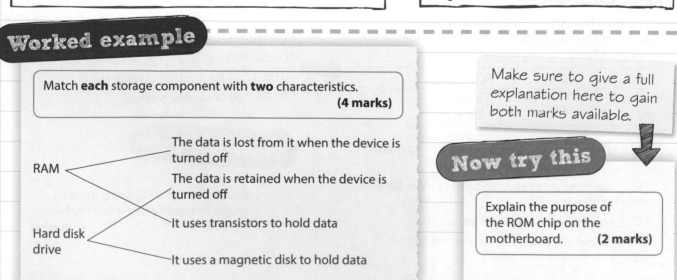

Make sure to give a full explanation here to gain both marks available.

Now try this

Explain the purpose of the ROM chip on the motherboard. **(2 marks)**

Mobile devices

Mobile devices are those which are portable – they can be easily carried around.

Features

Developers need to balance lots of different needs when they are designing a mobile device.

INCREASING POWER can DECREASE BATTERY LIFE, so developers have to balance customer needs.

Some of the important factors are:

- battery life
- size
- weight
- functionality (what it can do)
- interface.

Smartphones and tablets are examples of mobile devices.

Interface

The interface is the layout of the screen and how the user can interact with it. On a mobile device this is often a touch screen, so the interface needs to be different to a PC or laptop. For example, icons need to be big enough to press with a finger, rather than click with a mouse.

Components

Components in mobile devices are similar to those in, for example, a PC. In a PC, the processing is done in the CPU (and maybe the GPU).

Mobile devices use System on Chip (SoC). This combines the CPU and GPU into one chip. This is because they are smaller than PCs or laptops and therefore the components need to be more compact.

As technology has improved, the size of the devices has been made smaller – but also more powerful to provide more functionality. This includes apps such as taking and editing photos, and playing music and games.

Use the scenario to answer this question and think about all the factors to consider.

Worked example

What **five** things do you need to consider if developing a new mobile device?   **(5 marks)**

Size, weight, user interface, battery life, functionality

Now try this

Technology Visions want to create a new smartphone to rival the current ones on the market.

Describe **two** factors they need to consider when choosing components for the smartphone.   **(4 marks)**

Analogue and digital data

To transfer data it needs to be conveyed by either analogue or digital signals through cables or wireless. Data has to be converted to digital in order to be used by any devices or transferred over a network or the internet.

Analogue data is data that continuously varies. An example of this is human speech: sound waves travel through the air and can be heard by someone's ears. Analogue data includes non-digital music and any sounds produced in the environment.

Analogue data travels in a wave. It is drawn as a smooth wave. This represents how sound waves move through the atmosphere. They are smooth and continuous with no breaks in them.

Analogue sound wave

Digital data is data transmitted or stored using bits and bytes. The smooth analogue waves are sampled at regular intervals and simulate the sound waves.

Digital data is drawn in staggered waves. The computer fills in the gaps between the samples.

The more often the waves are sampled, the higher the quality of sound, as it is closer to the original analogue wave.

Digital sound wave

Analogue data is converted into digital data so it can be transferred across the internet.

Analogue

Digital

This image shows an analogue wave being sampled.

| Explain how a digital signal is created. | **(1 mark)** |

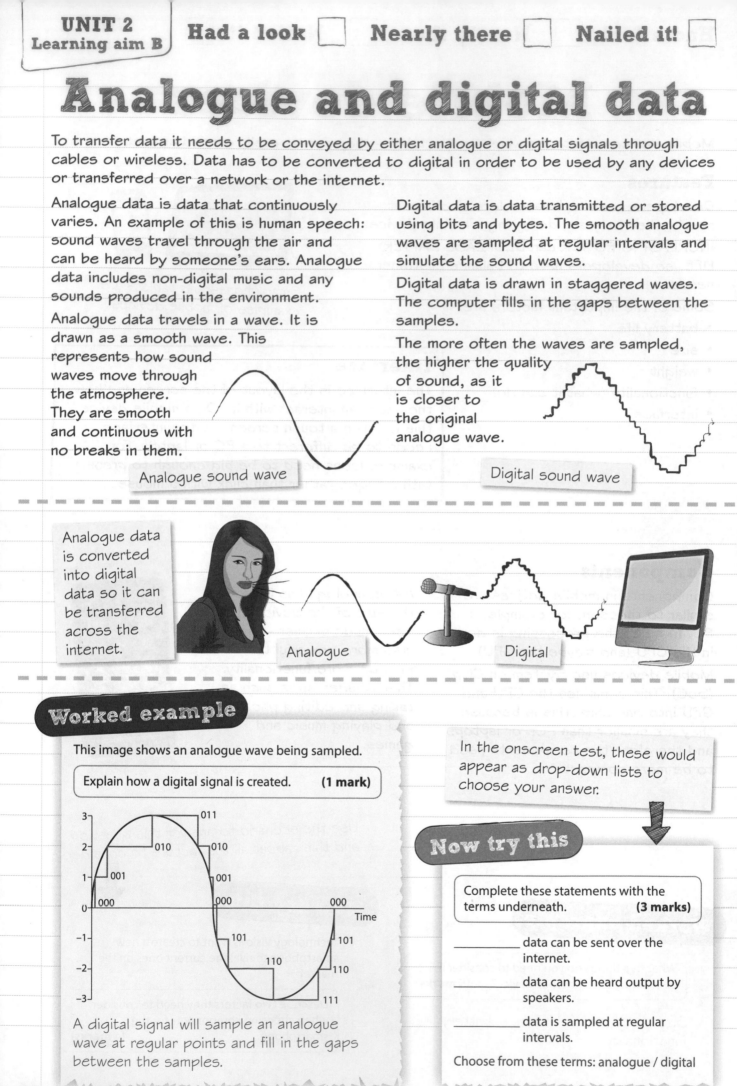

A digital signal will sample an analogue wave at regular points and fill in the gaps between the samples.

In the onscreen test, these would appear as drop-down lists to choose your answer.

Complete these statements with the terms underneath. **(3 marks)**

_____ data can be sent over the internet.

_____ data can be heard output by speakers.

_____ data is sampled at regular intervals.

Choose from these terms: analogue / digital

Converting denary to binary

Data is represented in binary notation.

Binary (base 2) counts in 1s and 0s. Base ten or denary is our whole number system that we use every day. The table below shows the denary (normal) numbers from 1 to 10 written in 4-bit binary which uses a binary number of four digits.

	8	4	2	1
0	0	0	0	0
1	0	0	0	1
2	0	0	1	0
3	0	0	1	1
4	0	1	0	0
5	0	1	0	1
6	0	1	1	0
7	0	1	1	1
8	1	0	0	0
9	1	0	0	1
10	1	0	1	0

Bits

A bit (binary digit) is a single character of data, either a 1 or 0. It is the smallest measurement of data.

Digital data is carried in pulses of energy around the components inside a digital device. Binary is represented by 1s and 0s, but is actually pulses of electricity which transfer data in a device.

Pulse of electricity = 1

No electricity = 0

In binary numbers the **place values** are different. Reading from right to left, the digits are worth 1, 2, 4, 8 and so on. Each column value doubles the value to the right.

How to convert from denary to binary

1. Draw a table with headings for each place value: 8, 4, 2 and 1.

2. Work out if the denary number fits into each heading number.
   If yes – write a 1 and take the remaining value to the next heading.

If no – write a 0 and take the whole number to the next heading.

$7 =$

8	4	2	1
0	1	1	1

= 0111

Repeat steps 2 and 3 using the remaining value and the next heading.

8 does not fit into 7   4 fits into 7, with 3 remaining   2 fits into 3, with 1 remaining   1 fits into 1

7 written in binary is 0111.

Your answer should be four digits written together e.g. 0101 – you can use rough paper to work it out if you wish.

Worked example

Convert these numbers into binary:
                (2 marks)

(a) 9   (b) 3

(a) 1001   (b) 0011

Now try this

Convert these numbers into binary.
                (2 marks)

(a) 1   (b) 8

Converting binary to denary

You can convert denary (normal numbers) to binary (base 2), as you saw on the previous page. You can also convert binary to denary. To do this you need eight headings instead of four and you complete the process in reverse order.

How to convert from binary to denary

1. Draw a table with eight headings 128, 64, 32, 16, 8, 4, 2 and 1

2. Write your binary number neatly underneath

3. Add up the headings of any column containing a 1

4. This gives you the denary (base 10) whole number of your 8-bit binary number.

(128)	64	32	(16)	8	(4)	(2)	1	
1	0	0	1	0	1	1	0	= 150

$10010110 = 128 + 16 + 4 + 2 = 150$

128	64	32	16	8	4	2	1	
0	1	1	0	1	1	0	1	= 109
1	1	1	1	1	1	1	1	= 255
0	0	1	0	0	0	0	1	= 33

Binary numbers are very small, even when used together in blocks of 8. We therefore have a way of measuring larger chunks of binary, which represent larger numbers. These are called 'Words'.

Word and word length

Word is a fixed number of bits e.g. 32-bits.

A word is the amount of data that can be processed in each clock cycle.

Word length is defined by the size of the processor.

Longer word length = more data processed = faster processor = faster computer

Binary Units

A byte is 8 bits.

You need to know the names of the different measurements and the order of their size.

Kilobyte	Kb	Thousand bytes	1024
Megabyte	Mb	Million bytes	1,000,000
Gigabyte	Gb	Thousand million bytes	1,000,000,000
Terabyte	Tb	Million million bytes	1,000,000,000,000
Petabyte	Pb	Thousand million million bytes	1,000,000,000,000,000

Now try this

Convert the following numbers into denary.   **(2 marks)**

Remember in the onscreen test there is a calculator which you can use.

(a) 01110101   (b) 10110000

Software

Software is a program or app which can run on a device that can process it. It allows the user to direct the operation of devices. There are two types of software: off-the-shelf and custom-made.

Off-the-shelf software

Software that can be purchased by anyone online or in shops. The specific program is the same for everyone.

Off-the-shelf software is made according to a standardized format.

Custom-made software (also known as bespoke)

Software that is specially designed and created for a particular purpose.
For example, a banking system or a production line.

This production line uses custom made software.

Advantages

Advantages of off-the-shelf software	Advantages of custom-made software
• Usually cheaper • Well tested and bug-free • Good support available from books and the internet and companies who make the product	• Specific to a particular function and company – does exactly what the company wants it to do

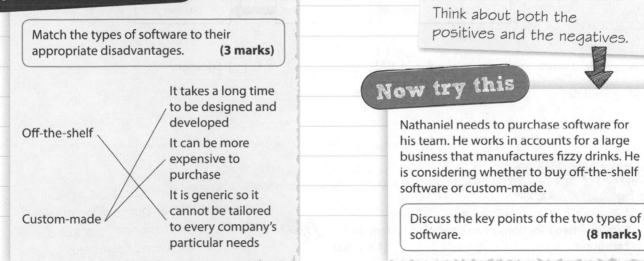

Worked example

Match the types of software to their appropriate disadvantages.   **(3 marks)**

Off-the-shelf

It takes a long time to be designed and developed

It can be more expensive to purchase

It is generic so it cannot be tailored to every company's particular needs

Custom-made

Think about both the positives and the negatives.

Now try this

Nathaniel needs to purchase software for his team. He works in accounts for a large business that manufactures fizzy drinks. He is considering whether to buy off-the-shelf software or custom-made.

Discuss the key points of the two types of software.   **(8 marks)**

55

Operating systems

An operating system is the software that links the hardware with the software.

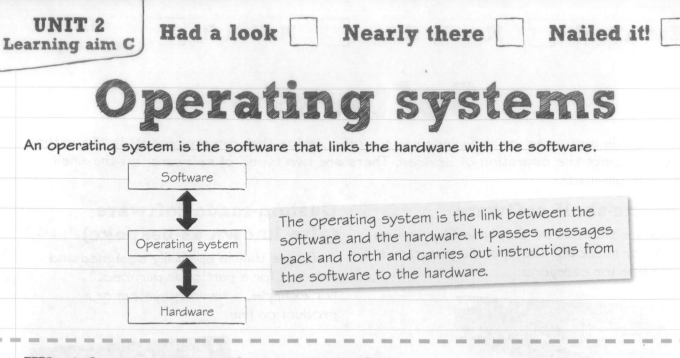

The operating system is the link between the software and the hardware. It passes messages back and forth and carries out instructions from the software to the hardware.

What does an operating system do?

1 File management – controls where data is saved and allows users to copy, rename, delete files and use folders.

2 Hardware management – loads programs, allocates resources to different programs, uses drivers to link specialist hardware (such as graphics).

3 Resource allocation – sends keyboard/mouse inputs to programs, as well as accessing other resources such as the printers and the hard disk drive.

4 Security – creates backups and access to files if there are multiple users.

Worked example

Saira is creating a digital scrapbook from printed photographs.

Choose **three** appropriate pieces of hardware she can use that the operating system will control.

(3 marks)

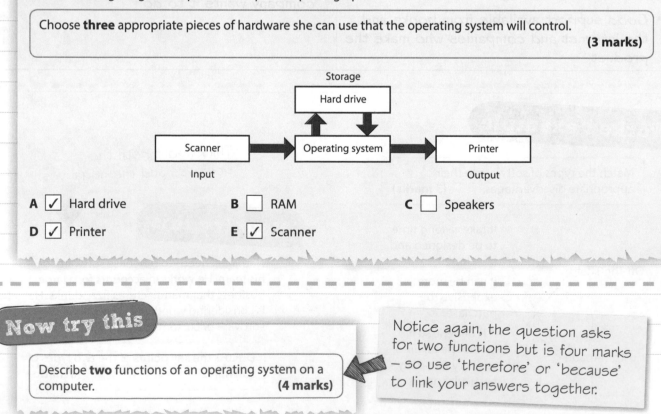

A ☑ Hard drive   **B** ☐ RAM   **C** ☐ Speakers

D ☑ Printer   **E** ☑ Scanner

Now try this

Describe **two** functions of an operating system on a computer.   **(4 marks)**

Notice again, the question asks for two functions but is four marks – so use 'therefore' or 'because' to link your answers together.

Utility applications

Utility applications are small programs which improve the performance of a device and usually only carry out one task. They can be software programs or built into the operating system.

There are lots of different types of utility applications – here are three examples:

1 Disk defragmenter (defrag)

Purpose: to make the hard disk drive run faster.

When a file is deleted, a gap is left on the hard disk drive. When a new file is saved, if it is too big for the gap, some is saved in the gap and the rest is saved elsewhere. Loading this file means it will need to be read in two different places, which takes longer. Over time this process makes the hard disk drive run slower. Defragmentation (defragging) rewrites the order of the files and puts them back together e.g. 'de-fragments'.

2 Software firewalls

Purpose: to prevent hackers and viruses from infecting a device.

Firewalls monitor data moving in and out of a device (or network) and block unwanted traffic, such as a virus.

3 Anti-virus software

Purpose: to prevent or remove viruses

Anti-virus software regularly scans the computer and connected devices for viruses. If any are found, it will remove or quarantine them.

Worked example

USER

(a) What type of software is a firewall? **(1 mark)**

A ☐ Productivity application
B ☐ Operating system
C ☑ Utility application

(b) Identify **two** functions of a firewall. **(2 marks)**

To monitor data between the user and the internet.

To block data which is not authorised.

Now try this

Using **one** example, explain the purpose of anti-virus as utility software. **(2 marks)**

Think about what the anti-virus needs to do.

User interfaces

An interface is the system which a user uses to interact with a device. There are graphical user interfaces (GUI) and command-line interfaces.

GUI (Graphical User Interface)

Microsoft® Windows® is an example of a Graphical User Interface

✓ Easy to use, therefore good for novice users

✓ Commands are presented onscreen in menus, buttons and toolbars

✓ Good for more visual software, such as web authoring

✓ Better accessibility – able to be used by users with less mobility who may struggle with a keyboard

✗ Runs slower than CLI because it has to process graphical information

✗ Slower to control than CLI because mouse and keyboard control takes more time than just keyboard control

CLI (Command-Line Interface)

UNIX® is an example of a Command-Line Interface

✓ Uses less system resources than GUI

✓ For experts, this is a fast interface to use, especially as it is all keyboard controlled rather than mouse

✗ Needs expertise

✗ User needs to remember the commands

Worked example

Identify the highlighted features of a GUI interface. **(3 marks)**

Icons to click on to start actions

Touch screen

Search box

Features of a GUI that make it easy for users to use

This tablet and mobile device have been designed to be accessible and easy to use. The features include:

• icons to click on to start actions
• a touch screen
• voice recognition
• magnifiers to make parts of the screen larger
• a 'home' button so the user can easily return to the main screen.

Think about ease of use – SuperTech will want to sell as many new phones as possible.

Now try this

SuperTech is developing a new smartphone. This will have a GUI touchscreen interface.

Describe **two** aspects they need to take into consideration when developing the interface of this new technology. **(4 marks)**

Software installation and upgrades

Software installation is saving a software program to permanent storage (like a hard disk drive) so that it can be used.

Software upgrade is to add extra functionality to a program or to completely replace it with a better program.

This may relate to the operating system or productivity applications.

ACCESSIBILITY FEATURES – Will it be used by users with additional needs?

SPEED – Is it fast enough, especially if it is new software run on older hardware, which affects efficiency and user experience?

COMPATIBILITY – Will it work with preferred applications and hardware?

Factors to consider when installing/ upgrading software

HARDWARE PLATFORM – Is the spec enough for the new software?

COST – Does the cost include the licence, set-up, training, maintenance?

SECURITY FEATURES – Does it include firewalls, malware management such as anti-virus, setting user permissions, user support?

Productivity applications

A productivity application is software that improves the efficiency of everyday tasks, for example writing a letter on a computer in word processing software. Here are some examples:

- Office software e.g. word processing, spreadsheets, databases, email, presentation software, desktop publishing
- Multimedia software e.g. graphics, web-authoring, video editing
- CAD/CAM

Worked example

Jonathan would like to buy two pieces of software, which are also available as a suite.

Identify **two** reasons for buying the suite of programs instead of individual programs.
(2 marks)

1 Saving money by buying them in bulk.

2 A common approach for all programs in the suite, makes them easier to learn.

Now try this

Shine Design is a creative company that creates websites for clients. A new version of their graphic software has been released and they would like to upgrade.

Explain **three** factors which they should consider before making this upgrade. **(6 marks)**

Think about the graphic software you have seen or used – they are often big programs that need high-spec devices.

Programming concepts

The hierarchy below shows the whole process of how a computer works. The languages create the software you see on-screen, which is eventually turned into the electricity moving through the hardware as on-and-off pulses.

Hierarchy structure of a computer system

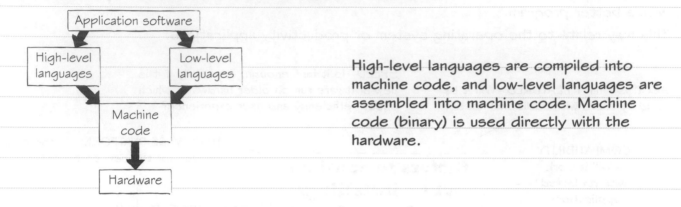

High-level languages are compiled into machine code, and low-level languages are assembled into machine code. Machine code (binary) is used directly with the hardware.

- **Application software:** Software shown on screen and used by the user. Has a user interface. Provides a function such as productivity, solving problems or entertainment.

- **High-level programming language:** A language which is closer to natural human language (than machine code). Examples include C++, C#, Java, Visual Basic. Needs to be compiled into machine code before it can be run.

- **Low-level programming language:** A language which is closer to machine code (than natural human language). They are written using an assembler.

- **Machine code:** Binary code that the computer understands.

- **Hardware:** The actual hardware of a computer, controlled by the CPU. Carries out each machine code instruction.

Worked example

Explain how a program written in a high-level language is carried out by the computer hardware. **(2 marks)**

A high-level language is very close to natural human language (English). To run high-level language it needs to be compiled by a compiler. This turns it into machine code, which is in binary. This can then be understood by the computer, including the processor, and the instructions carried out. The whole program has to be compiled before it can be run.

Remember to read the question carefully.

Now try this

How is a high level language turned into machine code? Tick **one** option from the following. **(1 mark)**

A ☐ Compiled

B ☐ Expanded

C ☐ Converted

D ☐ Compressed

Programming languages

High-level language

- Powerful and easy to understand
- Closer to natural human language (English), which makes it more intuitive
- Imperative – Tells the computer what to do step-by-step.
- Procedural – Has a definite start and end point. Runs through in a logical sequence.
- Event-driven – Waits ('listens') for events, such as a mouse click, then will carry out an action.
- Object-orientated – These view programs as a collection of objects, such as a database record, and not as a list of tasks as in procedural programming.

Low-level language

- Runs quickly as they do not need to be compiled
- Takes up less memory space
- Assembly language – A language which uses mnemonics but is very close to machine code. Turned into machine code using an assembler.
- Mnemonics – Abbreviations which are used in assembly language and are short instructions, e.g. MOV stands for move, CMP stands for compare.
- Machine Code – Binary code run directly by the CPU.

Worked example

Procedural programs used to be more common. After GUIs became standard for software, event programming became a more popular method of programming.

> Explain **one** reason why event programming has become more popular in recent years. **(2 marks)**

Event programming 'listens' for events such as a mouse click on a certain part of the screen and then actions will be carried out. A GUI allows the user to choose what they want to do using windows, icons and menus, which means it is based around the user carrying out events (like clicking on an icon). Procedural programs ran in sequence and could not be interrupted by an event until the sequence was complete. Therefore, as GUIs have become more popular, procedural programs are used less than event-driven.

Now try this

What type of language is shown in the box opposite? **(1 mark)**

A ☐ High-level

B ☐ Low-level

```
SUB32    PROC
         CMP AX,97
         JL DONE
         CMP AX,122
         JG DONE
         SUB AX,32
DONE:    RET
SUB32    ENDP
```

These abbreviations are known as mnemonics.

Flow charts 1

Flow charts are used to show what happens in a program. A flow chart is a useful tool when designing a program.

Flow chart symbols

You need to be able to recognise these five different types of symbol used in a flow chart.

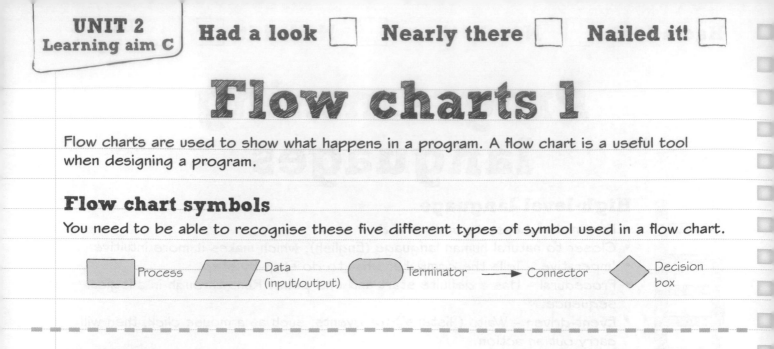

Process   Data (input/output)   Terminator   Connector   Decision box

Symbols used in flowcharts

Terminator	Start and finish of the program
Process	Calculation or operation
Decision box	Decision – leads to Yes or No branches
Data (I/O)	Take in data or give out data
Connector	Connects symbols together. Make sure the arrow is in the right direction (or both).

Worked example

A decision box always has two branches drawn from it. What are the labels?   **(1 mark)**

A ☐ True/False   B ☐ Match/No match

C ☑ Yes/No   D ☐ And/Or

Now try this

Draw the symbols in this flow chart.   **(4 marks)**

Put in the two terminators first, then the decision boxes. Then look for the data inputs and outputs.

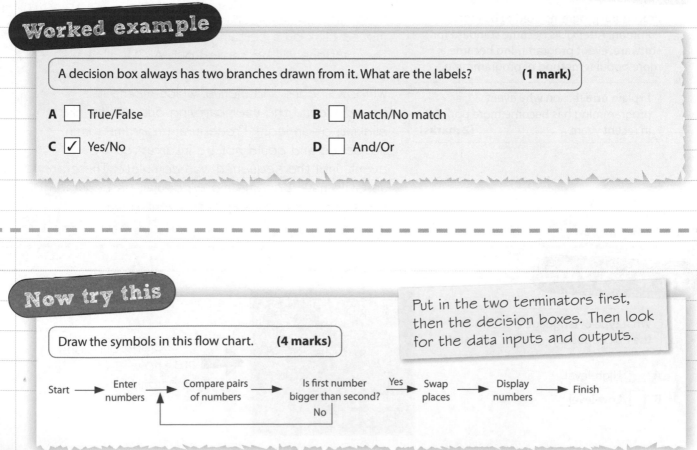

Start → Enter numbers → Compare pairs of numbers → Is first number bigger than second? — Yes → Swap places → Display numbers → Finish

No

Flow charts 2

Flow charts can be used to show process, for example to convert currency or calculate wages.

Flow charts and programming

Flow charts are used to plan programs. They help programmers work out the logic, what variables will be needed and the steps that are needed to make it work. A flow chart shows where the program starts, where decisions are taken, processing operations, inputs and outputs.

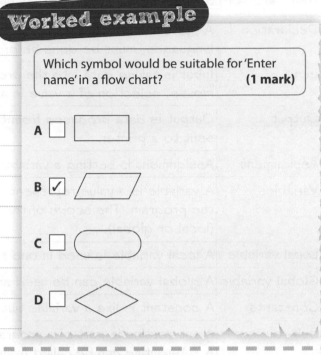

Worked example

Which symbol would be suitable for 'Enter name' in a flow chart? **(1 mark)**

A ☐ ▭

B ☑ ▱

C ☐ ⬭

D ☐ ◇

Now try this

(a) Mark has worked 35 hours this week. Using the flowchart, state what the flowchart output would be.

(b) Sharmeen has worked 20 hours and 10 hours overtime, state what the flowchart output would be.

Currency convertor

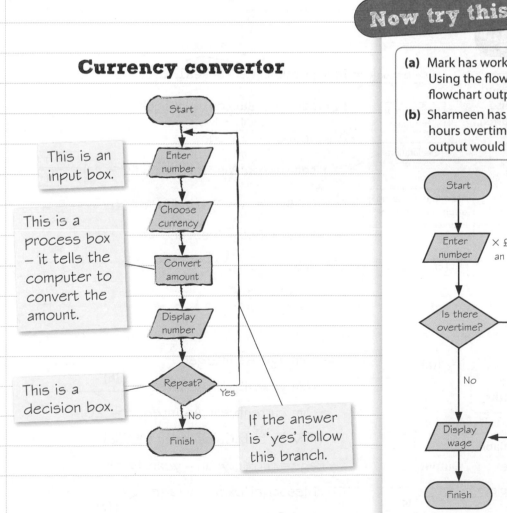

This is an input box.

This is a process box – it tells the computer to convert the amount.

This is a decision box.

If the answer is 'yes' follow this branch.

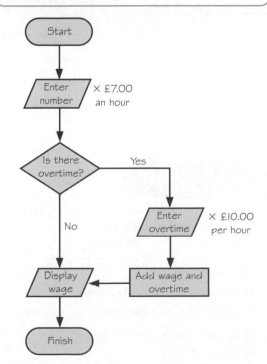

Programming – terminology

There are terms used in programming that have special meanings for this field of computing.

Declaration	A statement of a variable name, data type and sometimes initial value – in most languages, must be done before the variable is used.
Input	Input is taking data into the program. For example, this could be a click of the mouse, selection of a value in a combo box or a value typed into a textbox.
Output	Output is data produced from the program. This could be displayed on-screen or sent to a printer.
Assignment	Assignment is setting a variable to a value.
Variables	A variable is a value represented by a name. The value can be changed throughout the program. The scope of the variable is where it can be used in the program (local or global).
Local variable	A local variable is used in one sub-routine only.
Global variable	A global variable can be used anywhere in the program.
Constants	A constant is like a variable but is not changed; it is always the same, e.g. pi.
Sub-routines	A sub-routine is part of a program and allows the program to be broken into chunks. A sub-routine can be called from the main program as many times as needed.

Worked example

Identify **one** assignment and **one** global variable in this code. **(2 marks)**

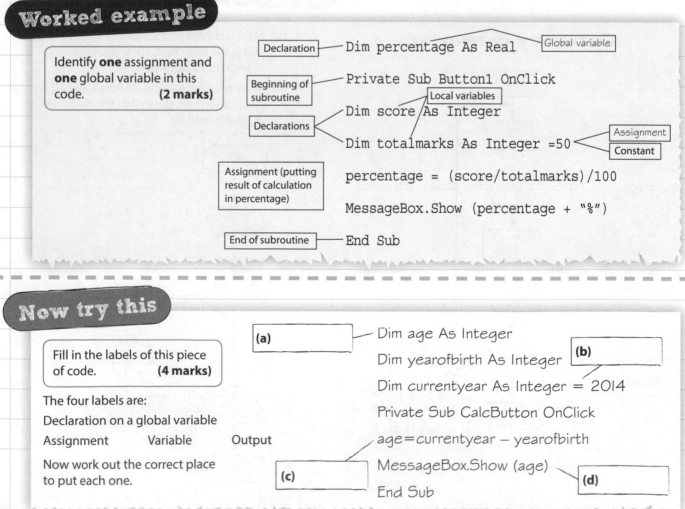

```
Dim percentage As Real              [Declaration] [Global variable]

Private Sub Button1 OnClick         [Beginning of subroutine]

Dim score As Integer                [Declarations] [Local variables]

Dim totalmarks As Integer =50       [Assignment] [Constant]

percentage = (score/totalmarks)/100  [Assignment (putting result of calculation in percentage)]

MessageBox.Show (percentage + "%")

End Sub                             [End of subroutine]
```

Now try this

Fill in the labels of this piece of code. **(4 marks)**

The four labels are:

Declaration on a global variable

Assignment   Variable   Output

Now work out the correct place to put each one.

```
(a) ─── Dim age As Integer
        Dim yearofbirth As Integer  (b)
        Dim currentyear As Integer = 2014
        Private Sub CalcButton OnClick
        age=currentyear – yearofbirth
(c) ─── MessageBox.Show (age)        (d)
        End Sub
```

Programming – data types

Data type defines the type of data which is to be stored by a variable.

Data types for programming

Data type	Description	Example
Character	A single letter or number	M
String	A combination of letters, numbers, symbols and spaces	Robert
Integer	A whole number	23
Real	A number with fractions	23.15
Boolean	True or false	True

Notice that these data types are different from the data types used in databases in Unit 1. They are similar, but have different names.

The data type is set so that the variable can perform actions. For example, an Integer can store a number that can be used in a calculation. A String could hold a number but could not be used in a calculation.

```
Dim salary As Integer
Dim weeklypay As Integer

weeklypay = salary / 52

MessageBox.Text ("Your weekly
pay is " + weeklypay)
```

This text calculates weekly pay from a yearly salary

Annotating code for maintenance

Code should be annotated for maintenance. This will make it easier for others to make changes at a later date. Changes may be needed to remove bugs that are found or upgrade the program to add more functionality.

Worked example

Suggest an appropriate data type for each variable. **(1 mark)**

CustomerName	Gender	Age
String	Character	Integer

Now try this

Krissie is a programmer who has developed a program for a retail business. She has now moved on to work for a different business.

Why is it good that she has thoroughly annotated her code? **(1 mark)**

Remember that annotating is putting comments in the code to explain what it does.

Programming – data structures

A data structure is an organisation that data fits into. Different structures are used for particular purposes and choosing the correct data structure is an important part of designing a program.

Records

- Records are like a database. They use tables and fields.
- A database is a collection of data.
- Data about one topic is stored in a table, e.g. information about all of the students in a school.
- A row in a table that stores data about a single item is a record, e.g. information about one student.
- The columns in a table store categories that are called fields, Name, Address, Gender, and Date of Birth.

> A 2D array can be used for a game of chess, which represents the two axes on the board. Each dimension can store an axis of the board.

Arrays

- An array is a type of variable that can hold several values (unlike a normal variable, which can only hold one at a time, e.g. score = 3). In simple terms they can be thought of as tables with a number of rows and columns.
- Each piece of data in an array is referred to by a number, which starts at 0 and marks the position of the data (see diagram below)
- The dimensions of the array are the different groups of data stored, e.g. 1D array has one group of data, 2D has two related groups, 3D has three related groups.

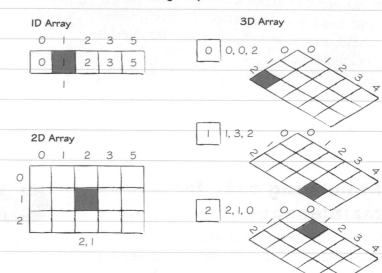

> Compare with the 2D array needed for a game of chess – how is a Rubik's® Cube different?

Worked example

What type of array would be used for a program simulating a Rubik's cube? **(1 mark)**

3D array

Now try this

A local gym is creating a program to store the data of their members.

Choose a suitable data structure. **(1 mark)**

A ☐ Variables
B ☐ 1D array
C ☐ 2D array
D ☐ Records

Exam skills 1

You will have I hour to complete the onscreen test. The test is worth 50 marks and will contain a variety of questions, including some multiple-choice questions.

Answering multiple-choice questions

✓ Make a note of the key words in the question.

✓ Read all the options carefully.

✓ Rule out the ones you know are wrong.

✓ Select what you think is the right answer.

✓ Double check the remaining options as well to make sure you are right.

Choosing the best answers

You need to be really careful when you are choosing your answers. There are often choices that look sensible, but aren't suitable for the CONTEXT of the question.

Always read the question carefully and choose the MOST APPROPRIATE options for the context.

Read the question carefully – notice how this question asks "which one of the following is NOT..." and is looking for the incorrect answer.

Worked example

Which **one** of the following is **not** a use of network systems?   **(1 mark)**

Click on **one** of the boxes.

A ☐ Sharing   B ☐ Entertainment

C ☑ Privacy   D ☐ Communication

Worked example

Select the correct explanation for these **two** terms operating in the CPU.   **(2 marks)**

ALU

Permanent storage for data

Store bytes of data while being calculated

Pass data to other components

Registers

Carry out calculations and comparisons

To answer this question, you would click on the term on the left then on the answer on the right – a line will appear connecting them.

Other possibilities for this type of question might include drag-and-drop from a selection of terms into blank boxes.

Exam skills 2

As well as multiple-choice questions, you will also have to answer some short-answer questions.

Answering short-answer questions

✓ Read the question carefully.

✓ Take note of key words.

✓ Note the number of marks available for the question.

✓ Make sure you make the same number of statements as there are marks available. For example, if the question is worth 2 marks, make at least two statements.

✓ Don't repeat words from the question. If you do, make sure you go on to explain in further detail using other words too.

✓ If an activity is referred to in the question, make sure your answers relate to this activity.

✓ The space provided for your answer will be a box where you can write as much as you want – remember to be detailed but concise.

✓ Ensure you use information and creative technology related examples as much as possible.

✓ If you have got time once you have finished answering all the questions, it's a great idea to make sure your answers make sense when read alongside the question.

Identify vs explain

Different questions have different command words. If a question asks you to IDENTIFY, it is asking for a simple statement, but if you are asked to EXPLAIN then make sure your answer is developed and that you give more than a simple statement. You should be using words like BECAUSE or THEREFORE, leading you to a more in-depth answer.

Compare and contrast

If a question asks you to compare and contrast the characteristics of different things, then you need to make sure that you discuss the characteristics of both. Using words like WHEREAS or HOWEVER will help to link two parts of the sentence together to show that you are meeting the command word.

Worked example

Jonathan would like to buy two pieces of software, which are also available as a suite.

> Identify **two** reasons for buying the suite of programs instead of individual programs. **(2 marks)**

To save money by buying them in bulk.

A common approach for all programs in the suite makes them easier to learn.

The command word in this question is 'identify'. This means your answer should be a simple sentence. The number of items you need to identify is given to you in this question. You can also use the number of marks available as a guide.

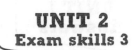
Exam skills 3

In your exam, you will have some extended-answer questions to complete. These can be based on any topic covered in the learning aims.

Answering extended-answer questions

Extended-answer questions will NOT have bullet points to guide you in your answer but each question will be phrased so that you can identify the required information for your response, if you know the subject area well.

- ✓ Take time to read the question carefully.
- ✓ Look for the key words in the question.
- ✓ Focus on those words that tell you what you need to write about.
- ✓ Do not just write bullet points!
- ✓ Do not simply repeat the words from the question without explaining them.

It is a very good idea to do a quick plan before you write your answer to make sure you cover the key points.

Key points to remember

For the extended-answer questions, unlike other types of question, you do not get a mark for every point you make. You are marked on your ability to:

- provide a full and balanced answer (which is why it is so important to identify the key words in a question)
- provide an answer that is well written and shows your full understanding of the topic in the question. Therefore, having identified the key words, it is essential that your response relates to all of them to achieve maximum marks.

Extended-answer questions can be based on any area of the unit. The extended-answer questions are designed to stretch you. A series of simple statements will not be enough for full marks.

Worked example

A car manufacturer uses robots on its production line and a primary school uses teachers. Discuss the difference between using humans or robots in these different organisations.

The car manufacturer uses robots because they can be programmed to carry out repetitive tasks and do not need breaks.

Another advantage for the car manufacturer could be that robots are very accurate.

The school uses humans for teachers because they have emotions and empathy and can respond to the children.

Another reason for using humans instead of robots for teachers is that they can make quick decisions, whereas a robot can only follow instructions.

A main difference between robots and humans in these organisations is that humans are adaptable and can deal with people; they can make changes if a situation needs it, whereas a robot will keep repeating the same error.

Plan your answer by jotting down each point you want to make. This will help you include everything in a logical order, in your answer.

The conclusion should be relevant to the case study and the points you have made.

69

Answers

The following pages contain answers to the 'Now try this' questions in Unit 1 of the Revision Guide. In many cases these are not the only correct answers.

Learning aim A

1. Online services 1

A Instant messaging

2. Online services 2

It is cheaper and quicker to download software because the company does not need to print and post the software on a DVD.

3. Online advertising

Banner and pop-up adverts capture the attention of the user because they are usually animated or include a video, or appear over the text the user is trying to read.

They can retain attention by targeting a specific audience, for example an advert for a website selling saddles on a horse-riding event website.

4. Online documents – file compression

(a) Compression will allow all of the files to be compressed into one file and makes the file smaller, allowing Sharmeen to send it by email.

(b) To compress a file, an algorithm is used and the last item of the file is an index.
To expand a file, the index allows the files to return to their original size.

5. Online software and backups

Online software can be accessed anywhere there is an internet connection so, for example, it can be used in the office or on the train.

Online software can be used on different devices, so a user can use it on a computer or mobile device and it will be the same on both.

6. Collaborative working online

(a) Version control is important so they know they are working on the most up-to-date version of the document.

(b) Keith and Shabina can use software which records the time and identity of the user working on the document (such as Track Changes) so they know when the latest changes were made.

7. Online communication 1

A business can use social networking microblogging to advertise their business and inform potential customers of the latest deals.

They could also use social networking to create a network of customers who like their products, for example using a site like Facebook. They could offer customers exclusive deals.

8. Online communication 2

Instant messaging requires those involved to be connected at the same time, using email does not. The messages are sent instantly across the internet, whereas in email they sit on the server until they are accessed.

9. Voice over Internet Protocol

VoIP can allow people who work in different countries to communicate – it can save time and money by holding meetings over VoIP instead of face-to-face.

It uses internet only so there is no additional cost (unlike phone calls)

VoIP is also cheaper than travelling and hiring a venue, because users can stay where they are to communicate.

10. Cloud computing

Advantages include:

- cost, because you can buy a cheaper computer with a smaller hard drive
- availability, because it can be accessed anywhere where there is an internet connection.

11. Ubiquitous computing

One example of where ubiquitous computing could be useful is in stock control where items are scanned to record how many are in a warehouse. Another example could be where RFID chips are put into pets so they can be reunited with their owners if they are lost.

Learning aim B

12. The internet – hardware

D Router

13. The internet – network diagrams

Client – ISP

14. The internet – connection methods

Low bandwidth would make the website run slowly. This is because less data can move through the cable (less bits per second), therefore the data is moving more slowly.

15. The internet – protocols

B FTP

(You can rule out HTML as a protocol name will finish with a P for Protocol!)

16. World Wide Web

The user requests a web page by using its web address (URL). A copy is downloaded from the web server onto the client's computer. It is displayed using a web browser.

17. HTML

<a href="http://www.penguins.com"><img="penguins.jpg"></a>

18. URLs

Protocol – domain name – path

19. Search engines

A user types key words into the search engine. All the time web crawlers are searching the internet for new or updated web pages and adding what they find into the search engine's database. The database is searched for the user's keywords. The results are displayed in order of popularity with sponsored links at the top.

20. Email – purposes and uses

Emails can be delivered to multiple recipients at the same time; for example they could email all of their customers at the same time with a new deal.

A disadvantage could be security because all emails are at risk from viruses that can be spread through email.

21. Email – protocols

SMTP is a 'push' protocol because it pushes the email from the server to the client.

POP3 is a 'pull' protocol because it pulls the email from the server to the client when requested.

22. Data exchange – packet switching

One advantage is security because the data is sent by different routes, if a hacker intercepts a packet, they will only obtain a section of the data, rather than all of it.

Another advantage is that the data will transmit quicker than if it was sent all in one file because smaller files travel more easily through network cables than larger ones.

A disadvantage is that if there is a problem during transmission, the packets may not be compiled correctly at the other end and the data will be corrupted.

23. Data exchange – transmission modes

C it transfers several bits at the same time.

24. Wired transmission methods

Fibre optic cable ————⟶ Fast, expensive

UTP ————————⟶ Cheap

Coaxial ——————⟶ Slow, low capacity

25. Wireless transmission methods

A The printer is a long way away from the computer.

C The printer is near a kitchenette where there is a kettle and a microwave.

26. Client-side processing

Client-side processing may use the client's computer's clock because it will be accurate to their time zone (different for different users around the world) and accurate to the time which is seen on the user's screen.

27. Server-side processing

(a) Server-side processing is where the processing of a web page occurs on the web server rather than the client's machine. It is created using web scripts. An example is a web form that has been filled in and submitted for processing.

(b) One benefit is efficiency, because it is processed on the server rather than needing to download it onto the client.

Another benefit is that it is browser independent, because it doesn't matter what browser the user is using as it occurs on the web server.

One disadvantage is security, because moving data over a network puts it at risk to threats such as hackers.

Another disadvantage is overloading, because if too many demands are put on the server it may run slowly or crash.

28. Database theory

A primary key which appears in another table is a foreign key. This creates a relationship between the two tables and allows them to connect. For example, you can search for a product in a product table and also the related supplier in a supplier table.

29. Databases in practice

(a) A local database can be accessed by users on that particular network.

(b) An online database can be accessed over the internet.

Learning aim C

30. Threats to data

One threat which can affect a business could be a computer virus, which is a malicious program that can damage or steal data.

A second threat could be accidental damage, which could include floods and fires.

31. Protection of data

Any two of the following:

- Computer viruses are malicious programs which replicate and can damage or steal data. Anti-virus software can be used to scan for infected files and delete the virus or quarantine the infected files.
- Phishing emails are a threat because they pretend to be from a legitimate sender and try to trick you into clicking a link or revealing your personal details. To protect against phishing emails, users should use good practice and common sense and be alert for indicators of a fake email.
- Hackers are people who try to access areas of a network without authorisation. A firewall can protect against hackers because it monitors data going in and out of a network and can prevent hackers from gaining access.
- An opportunist threat might be a person who finds an unattended computer that has been logged into a system and they decide to use it to access unauthorised data. This could be prevented with physical security such as locks on the doors, CCTV and ensuring computers are locked or logged off when not in use.

32. Legislation

B He has broken UK law because he is making money from his café.

D He is likely to be fined under the Copyright, Designs and Patents Act 1988.

The following pages contain answers to the 'Now try this' questions in Unit 2 of the Revision Guide.

Learning aim A

36. Technology systems

Companies in the construction sector could use CAD (computer aided design) software to make accurate design blueprints. They could also use spreadsheet software to track finances on a construction project.

37. Issues in technology systems

Customers who buy online can have a positive effect on the environment because they do not have to travel to the store, therefore reducing the amount of pollution put into the atmosphere from their vehicles. However, the products still need to be transported from the supplier to the business and from the business to the customer, which will create pollution from the vehicles.

38. Developing technology systems

One advantage could be reduced costs, for example if they can manufacture the packaging more cheaply, perhaps using robots, which could mean lower costs and higher profits.

Another advantage could be improved performance, for example if the design software is easier to use, the designers will be able to create better designs and it may improve their work experience.

39. Hardware devices

A programmable digital device is anything with a digital control, such as a washing machine that may have a digital display and buttons instead of dials to choose the settings. It will probably have extra features, such as calculating how long a wash will take. The purpose of these types of devices is to control and add better functionality to everyday items, such as microwaves and cars.

40. Input and output

C Microphone

41. Storage

(a) A USB memory stick is a type of SSD (solid state drive) as it has no moving parts. This means it is a quicker and quieter type of storage (compared to those which use magnetic disks). It is also portable, which means it can be removed from the computer and carried to a different computer in another place. In addition, USB is a common type of socket found in most computers and laptops, and some games consoles.

(b) USB memory sticks are portable and small so they can be fragile and quite easily broken, which means Sadia could lose her coursework. In addition, they have a relatively small capacity (although available in increasingly bigger data sizes) therefore, if her coursework includes lots of images or videos, she may need to use a storage method with a bigger capacity.

42. Automated systems

(a) Input: barcode scanner, touchscreen
(also PIN pad, money/note receptacle, card reader)

(b) Output: printer (receipt), screen
(also lights, speakers)

43. Devices to capture data

Sheppard Airways new self-check-in machine can use a magnetic strip reader for passengers' credit cards, although they should also include a facility for Chip & PIN and contactless payments.

They could use an Optical Mark Reader for scanning passengers' boarding passes. These could have a pattern printed on them which could be translated into information about their flight time, airline, destination, etc.

44. Types and uses of networks

WAN = The internet

LAN = A network in a university

PAN = A smartphone being synched with a PC

45. Benefits of networks

(a) A printer, data or other similar answers.

(b) Networks allow data and resources to be shared. In an office, this would mean that only one printer is needed instead of buying one printer for each user. This would save money. The users in the office could also share data so they could work collaboratively and more efficiently. Their data would be safer as they can access files from their network rather than sharing them on portable storage, such as USB memory sticks.

46. Methods of transferring data

Answer version 1:

Jack could choose to use a wired method for his LAN. Using cables (instead of wireless) can be more reliable for his network, meaning the users are less likely to lose their network connection. He could use STP (shielded twisted pair) cables because these are the cheapest (compared to coaxial and fibre optic). However, because they are shielded (rather than unshielded in UTP), this gives more protection from interference. He would not need fibre optic as this is too expensive for a LAN of five users.

Answer version 2:

Jack could choose to use a wireless method for his LAN. Using wireless (instead of wired) means that his users have more freedom to move around the office and could use laptops and tablets instead of desktop PCs. He could use Wi-Fi for his network and he would need to include a WAP (Wireless Access Point) for his users to connect to and make sure each device had wireless connectivity.

Learning aim B

47. Main components of a computer

B RAM

48. Processing digital data 1

ALU = Does comparisons and calculations with bits of data

Register = Stores bytes of data that are used by the ALU and also the results

Control unit = Passes data to the RAM and other components

49. Processing digital data 2

Data can be put into the cache memory quickly from the fast RAM and then transferred more slowly into the HDD. This allows the RAM to move onto other data more quickly.

50. Memory and storage

ROM is a type of memory chip that is fixed to the motherboard. It knows the date, time and boot-up sequence of the computer. When the power button is pressed, electricity is sent to the ROM chip and it initiates the computer's boot-up sequence.

51. Mobile devices

Answers may include two of the following:

• Battery life – they need to make sure the new features do not drain the battery too quickly.

• Size and weight – customers will expect a phone of similar or smaller size and weight to other phones on the market, so their new technology must be small and light.

• Functionality – it will be expected that a new smartphone can do more things than other phones on the market.

52. Analogue and digital data

Digital data can be sent over the internet.

Analogue data can be heard output by speakers.

Digital data is sampled at regular intervals.

53. Converting denary to binary

(a) 0001

(b) 1000

54. Converting binary to denary

(a) 117

(b) 176

Learning aim C

55. Software

Off-the-shelf software is generic, which means it is the same for everyone who buys it. This can make it cheaper and it will also have better support and fewer bugs. However, it may not do everything Nathaniel needs it to do. Off-the-shelf accounts software may have lots of features, but may not be suitable for his company's products, for example it may not let him store product prices for different sizes of fizzy drinks in litres.

Custom-made software (also known as bespoke) is specially designed for the purpose and will do everything Nathaniel needs it to do, and can even be made in the company's colours and with their logo. However, custom-made software can take a long time to create and is expensive.

56. Operating systems

An operating system manages the files in a computer. It allows users to save files, copy, rename and delete files and use folders.

It also manages the resources in a computer and controls the input and output devices. For example, it will take input from a keyboard and mouse and (once processed) display the result onscreen.

57. Utility applications

Utility software are small programs with one particular purpose. Anti-virus software will scan storage, such as a hard disk drive and USB memory sticks, looking for infected files. When it finds them it will delete the virus or quarantine the file.

58. User interfaces

SuperTech need to consider accessibility so that users with additional needs (such as poor eyesight) can also use the phone, for example, being able to magnify the images and words onscreen or having voice recognition. They should also consider ease of use, as customers will have an expectation that the smartphone is intuitive to use so that they can use it straight away without reading a manual.

59. Software installation and upgrades

Shine Design should consider the cost of the software because if it is very expensive they may need to put up their prices to pay for it and that may put customers off using them.

They should also consider the hardware they want to install it on as it may not be powerful enough and it may run slowly, which would make it frustrating to use, or they may need to buy new computers for it, which will increase the cost.

Additionally they should consider accessibility features as they may have employees who have additional needs and need to be able to use the new software as well.

60. Programming concepts

A Compiled

61. Programming languages

B Low-level

62. Flow charts 1

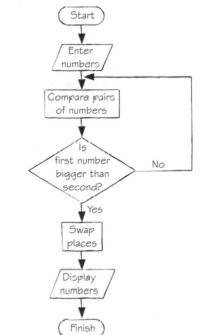

63. Flow charts 2

(a) £245 (b) £240

64. Programming – terminology

(a) Declaration on a global variable
(b) Assignment
(c) Variable
(f) Output

65. Programming – data types

It is good that Krissie has annotated her code because it will make it easier for her replacement to maintain her program. If the new programmer needs to make changes, they will find it easier to understand.

66. Programming – data structures

D Records

Your own notes

Your own notes

Revision is more than just this Guide!

You can get even more practice on each topic you revise with our corresponding Revision Workbook.

1-to-1 page match with this Revision Guide.

Guided questions help build your confidence.

Questions get you ready for your assessment test.

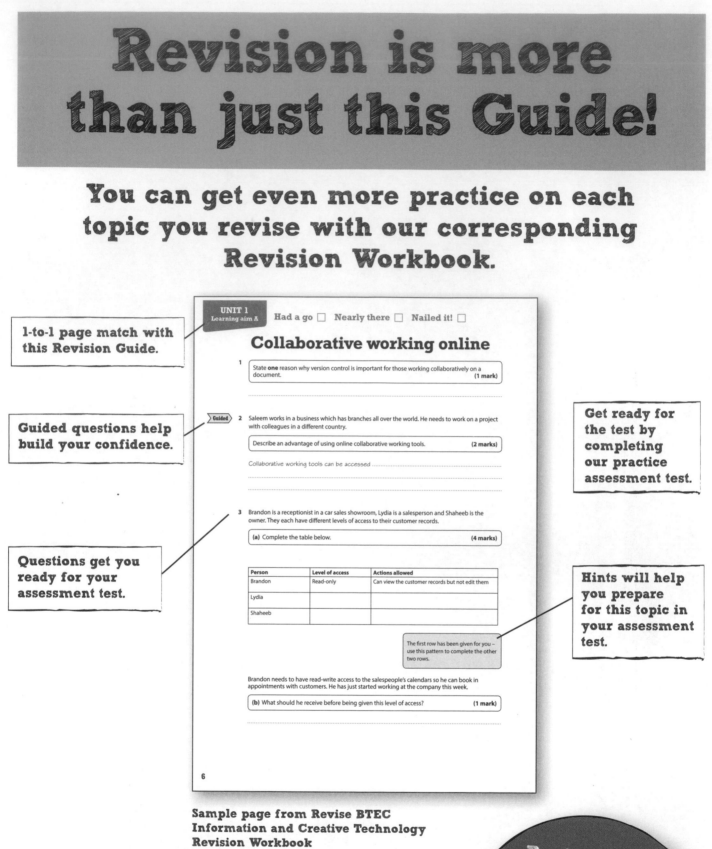

Get ready for the test by completing our practice assessment test.

Hints will help you prepare for this topic in your assessment test.

Sample page from Revise BTEC Information and Creative Technology Revision Workbook

Check out the matching Revision Workbook